Photo by Lisa Ebright
Amy Morton and Kyle Colerider-Krugh in a scene from The Goodman
Theatre production of "Sin." Set design by Scott Bradley.

SIN

BY WENDY MacLEOD

★

DRAMATISTS
PLAY SERVICE
INC.

SIN
Copyright © 1998, by Wendy MacLeod
ALL RIGHTS RESERVED

SPECIAL NOTE

SPECIAL NOTE ON SONGS AND RECORDINGS

DEDICATION

In memory of Soo-Z Matthews

SIN was produced by Second Stage Theatre (Carole Rothman, Artistic Director; Suzanne Schwartz Davidson, Producing Director) in New York City, in October, 1995. It was directed by David Petrarca; the set design was by Scott Bradley; the lighting design was by Robert Christen; the costume design was by Allison Reeds; the original music and sound design were by Rob Milburn; the production stage manager was Nancy Harrington; and the stage manager was Elaine Bayless. The cast was as follows:

AVERY .... Kelly Coffield
FRED .... Tom Aulino
LOUIS .... Julio Monge
MICHAEL .... Bruce Norris
JONATHAN .... Steve Carell
HELEN .... Camryn Manheim
JASON .... John Elsen
GERARD .... Jeffrey Hutchinson

SIN received its premiere at The Goodman Theatre (Robert Falls, Artistic Director; Roche Schulfer, Executive Director) in Chicago, Illinois, on October 31, 1995. It was directed by David Petrarca; the set design was by Scott Bradley; the costume design was by Allison Reeds; the lighting design was by Robert Christen; the sound design and original music were by Rob Milburn; the dramaturg was Susan V. Booth; and the production stage manager was Kimberly Osgood. The cast was as follows:

AVERY .... Amy Morton
MAN (LUST) .... Tim Rhoze
MICHAEL (SLOTH) .... David Pasquesi
DATE (GREED) .... Steve Carell
HELEN (GLUTTONY) .... Karen Vaccaro
FRED (ENVY) .... Kyle Colerider-Krugh
JASON (WRATH) .... Steve Pickering
GERARD, AVERY'S BROTHER (PRIDE) .... Jeffrey Hutchinson

SIN received a workshop production at Arena Stage (Doug Wager, Artistic Director) in Washington, D.C., in January, 1994. It was directed by Laurence Maslon.

CAST OF CHARACTERS

AVERY, a woman, 31, a Traffic Watcher for a local radio station
MAN (Lust), a poet
MICHAEL (Sloth), her estranged husband, a doctor
DATE (Greed), a Yuppie, 30s
HELEN (Gluttony), 32, her friend and roommate
FRED (Envy), her co-worker
JASON (Wrath), her boss
GERARD (Pride), her brother

TIME

Immediately before, during, and after the San Francisco earthquake, October, 1989.

SETTING

San Francisco.

A bar, a restaurant, Helen's apartment, a helicopter, Jason's office, a hospital room, a parking garage, Helen's car, a devastated street in the Marina District.

NOTE: Like in the medieval theater places are suggested by "mansions," a single suggestive prop.

SIN

ACT ONE

Sound of helicopter. Avery stands against the sky.

AVERY.   Have you ever flown over your own house? And seen your house, your yard, your car in the driveway. And you see a house that looks so happy. All the houses look happy from the sky. I like to see the houses in the early morning and watch the lights come on one by one. I imagine the sound of the newspaper on the porch, the smack of the hand on the alarm clock, the first sleepy leg draped over the body beside it. But I know the houses aren't like that. The newspaper never lands on the porch, the alarm doesn't go off, and the sleepy leg reaches for someone who isn't there anymore. The houses could be happy if people would just stop. Just stop being bad and start being good. Why do people act so stupid? I try to fix the world, but it wears me out. The world doesn't seem to want to change. The world doesn't seem to want to listen to me. From the sky, the world is perfect.

BLACKOUT

In the dark we hear the whir of a helicopter and the following voices. A radio is illuminated from within.

FRED.   A man. A woman. A cockpit. Meet George Jetson, his wife Elroy....
AVERY.   His wife wasn't Elroy.
FRED.   Who was she?
AVERY.   I don't remember. But it wasn't Elroy.
FRED.   Any Jetsons fans out there? Give us a call. And you'll win? What will they win, Avery?

AVERY.   A prize?

FRED.   A date with Avery Bly on High!

AVERY.   I'm married.

FRED.   Separated.

AVERY.   We still have a three-lane Bay Bridge westbound heading into San Francisco, traffic is backed up all the way to the Army Base Overpass....

FRED.   How long has it been now, Avery, five, six months?

AVERY.   Fred?

FRED.   Time to get back out there. Look out, San Francisco, traffic-watching babe breaking out!

AVERY.   Fred?

FRED.   A-oh!

AVERY.   Alternate routes? (*In the dark, a song like "I Feel the Earth Move"* blares.*)

Scene 1

Bar. Lust. Sloth. Avery sits alone at the bar.

MAN.   Did you feel the tremors?

AVERY.   I'm sorry.

MAN.   The tremors.

AVERY.   When?

MAN.   This morning. 7:46. Pacific time.

AVERY.   No.

MAN.   Must have been on bedrock.

AVERY.   I was in the air actually.

MAN.   Why?

AVERY.   It doesn't matter.

MAN.   It matters to me. You matter to me.

AVERY.   I'm waiting for someone.

MAN.   Aren't we all?

AVERY.   I'm really waiting for someone.

* See Special Note on Songs and Recordings on copyright page.

MAN.   Your sweetie?

AVERY.   My husband.

MAN.   You're not wearing a ring.

AVERY.   Men don't. A lot of men don't. Why should a woman?

MAN.   Because a wedding ring says hands off.

AVERY.   I can say hands off.

MAN.   I wish you wouldn't.

AVERY.   You're hitting on me because I'm the only woman here.

MAN.   Don't be so hard on yourself.

AVERY.   I'm not ... forget it.

MAN.   I'm hitting on you because you have the most beautiful smile I've ever seen.

AVERY.   Look. If it's true there were tremors this morning then the big one may be coming and if it's coming it may be as soon as tomorrow morning and if it comes tomorrow morning it may be my last morning on Earth and I certainly don't want to spend it in some stranger's apartment on a mattress on the floor in polyester blend sheets with the smell of dirty socks in the air. I don't want to spend my last morning on Earth with some stranger's jism trickling down my thigh wondering if he ever went through a period when he was confused about his preferences, nor do I want to spend it smelling somebody's morning breath as they apologize for having to rush off, assuring me there's a bagel in the freezer.

MAN.   You've done this before, then? *(Man smiles. Avery crosses away. Michael enters.)*

MICHAEL.   It's the Traffic Girl. Doo doo de doo doo. It's 6:55 and heeere's Avery Bly on High with the traffic.

AVERY.   I'm the Traffic Watcher. Not the Traffic Girl. They changed that.

MICHAEL.   Right. I understand women are voting now.

AVERY.   You're late.

MICHAEL.   Am I? That's news to me.

AVERY.   Maybe you should get a watch.

MICHAEL.   Oh I don't believe in all that.

AVERY.   They have sundials now, that you can wear on your wrist.

9

MICHAEL. Do they? I'd wear one of those. In a minute.

AVERY. It wouldn't work for you. You're never in the sun. You're always in bars.

MICHAEL. Patently untrue. Just last night I was....

AVERY. Where?

MICHAEL. Somewhere else.

AVERY. With a woman?

MICHAEL. Oh you don't have to worry about that. I'm too bereft for that. My manhood is more or less inert.

AVERY. You said you had something to tell me....

MICHAEL. I have many things to tell you. In my mind, I keep lists of things to tell you. There's a rather large category I call THINGS I MUST REMEMBER TO TELL AVERY. I must remember to tell her to rotate her tires and stay away from shellfish and....

AVERY. Michael.

MICHAEL. That I've been thinking about going to a meeting.

AVERY. Does that mean you're going to a meeting?

MICHAEL. Well, you have to place that in a cultural context. For me, a Catholic, the idea is equivalent to the act. If I think of going to a meeting, then, in a sense, I have gone to a meeting.

AVERY. If you would really go, that would make me so happy.

MICHAEL. That is no mean feat, making you happy. It's been so long since I've made you happy. Did I ever make you happy?

AVERY. You know you did.

MICHAEL. Do I?

AVERY. Michael, I would give anything to have you back....

MICHAEL. Jesus, just say the word....

AVERY. The way you were....

MICHAEL. This is the way I was. I think what you're looking for is the me you imagined me to be, or the me I might be in a perfect world....

AVERY. I'm looking for what you *could* be without this ... monkey on your back.

MICHAEL. Excuse me, but that's my monkey and nobody

10

insults my monkey, the last man who insulted my monkey ended up in the … doesn't that actually refer to a heroin addiction? … in the street, I mean, and I consider you a sort of expert on the street. Would you like another Coke? *(Michael flips through his wallet.)*

AVERY.   I'm fine.

MICHAEL.   *(Showing an empty wallet.)* Look at that. I thought I had a … do you think you can spare any cash?

AVERY.   Why do you need money?

MICHAEL.   I can't seem to remember my ATM code for some reason, I know it's one of my childhood pets but I can't seem to remember which one. It can't be Ribbons, can it?

AVERY.   Michael, did you get fired?

MICHAEL.   Did I ever tell you about Ribbons? Wonderful dog. Springer spaniel. He died the day I left for New Haven.

AVERY.   Oh my God, you got fired. What did they fire you for?

MICHAEL.   What do you think?

AVERY.   Drinking urine samples?

MICHAEL.   Drinking ur … that's doesn't make any sense, there's no alcohol content in urine. Patients complained. They smelled liquor on my breath. Can you believe that? The lies people tell.

AVERY.   Is there any chance they'll take you back?

MICHAEL.   There would be little to no chance. Nobody seems to want to take me back.

AVERY.   Well, do you think you can get another job? I mean, are you looking for another job?

MICHAEL.   No.

AVERY.   What do you do all day?

MICHAEL.   I've been extremely busy with my anti-metric campaign. You want to hear our slogan?

AVERY.   No.

MICHAEL.   "Give it to me in inches please."

AVERY.   Is that supposed to be dirty?

MICHAEL.   Would you like to hear our theme song? Perhaps you know it. "I Love You a Bushel and a Peck."

AVERY.   What's a peck?

11

MICHAEL.   See! It's happening already. We're losing our heritage. Our forefathers' measures. The old measurements were based on a man's foot.

AVERY.   I don't give a damn about the metric system.

MICHAEL.   Well you should. Your tax dollars are being spent to change all the signs.

AVERY.   What signs?

MICHAEL.   The signs, all the signs, the highway signs! Into kilometers.

AVERY.   Don't you miss working?

MICHAEL.   Don't I miss ... really Avery. If someone came to you and offered you whatever, big money, buckets of money, and said you never had to go up in that helicopter again, wouldn't you be ecstatic?

AVERY.   I won't be in the helicopter forever. I'll move up.

MICHAEL.   To where? Heaven?

AVERY.   To a better job.

MICHAEL.   You'll go to heaven, mark my words, because the thing about you is, you have integrity. You don't have any fun, but you do have integrity.

AVERY.   I have fun.

MICHAEL.   When?

AVERY.   I had fun with you.

MICHAEL.   That's because I did all the sinning for you. You had all the pleasure of sin without the eternal damnation. Who wouldn't have fun?

AVERY.   You don't have to be eternally damned.

MICHAEL.   I have a Bible, thank you. I stole it from the last motel room.

AVERY.   They'll just put out another.

MICHAEL.   The Gideons?

AVERY.   Yes.

MICHAEL.   Who are the Gideons? And how often do you suppose they come around?

AVERY.   Too often?

MICHAEL.   Congratulations Avery Bly, you have hit the daily double! Answer this question correctly and you'll be taking home a slightly used M.D.!

AVERY.   I don't want a slightly used M.D.

MICHAEL.   What do you call a bunch of dolphins? I repeat, what do you call a bunch of dolphins?

AVERY.   I want a sober M.D.

MICHAEL.   Answer the question or you'll have to forfeit five hundred dollars!

AVERY.   A pod.

MICHAEL.   Is that right? That doesn't sound right.

AVERY.   A pod.

MICHAEL.   That's something to do with plants.

AVERY.   A bunch of dolphins is a pod.

MICHAEL.   I'm sure you're right. You're always right. You're a very bright woman and that is the source of all your problems.

AVERY.   You've got a lot of nerve telling me what my problem is.

MICHAEL.   On the contrary. I'm an authority. Who better to talk to about problems than the original problem man? The root of all problems himself ... Dr. Michael Bannon. *(Makes a canned applause sound by cupping his mouth.)*

AVERY.   I have to go.

MICHAEL.   Don't go.

AVERY.   I hate it here. I hate bars.

MICHAEL.   Then it truly seems we must part.

AVERY.   We have parted.

MICHAEL.   I didn't agree to that.

AVERY.   Unless you're serious about going for help. It's an illness ... surely you....

TOGETHER.   Of all people.

MICHAEL.   I know all that illness stuff. The thing is, they used to think homosexuality was an illness....

AVERY.   That's an absurd comparison....

MICHAEL.   Bear with me, they used to think homosexuality was an illness and then of course they realized that there were millions of people perfectly happy sleeping with people of their own sex, so they said it *wasn't* an illness and then all these people who were considered sick were now considered well and they thrived.

13

AVERY.   They didn't thrive.

MICHAEL.   In an emotional sense....

AVERY.   They are not thriving! They're dying!

MICHAEL.   Well it's not my fault!

AVERY.   It's not their fault either.

MICHAEL.   I never said it was! Goodness gracious, Miss Bee in Her Bonnet, what was all that about? Did you just come from the hospital?

AVERY.   Yes.

MICHAEL.   How is your brother?

AVERY.   How do you think? Thank you for inviting me to this living wake. *(Avery turns to leave.)* And you won't be able to call me in the middle of the night anymore. I'm getting an unlisted number.

MICHAEL.   Oh? What is it?

AVERY.   Good-bye Michael.

MICHAEL.   Avery!

AVERY.   What?

MICHAEL.   Money? *(Avery puts five dollars on the bar.)* That's not enough.

AVERY.   It's happy hour.

MICHAEL.   Is it? That would explain the delirium, the ecstasy, the ... *(Avery starts to leave.)* I'm hungry.

AVERY.   Do they have food here?

MICHAEL.   Do they ... I come here for the food! Look there, they have nachos, potato skins, cheeseburgers, why it's practically a health food restaurant.

AVERY.   What do you want?

MICHAEL.   What do *you* want?

AVERY.   Nothing.

MICHAEL.   A Diet Coke for dinner! Say a prayer for her, girls.

AVERY.   I'll be eating later.

MICHAEL.   Lean Cuisine?

AVERY.   What?

MICHAEL.   Isn't that what you single gals eat? A plastic baggie chock full of low-calorie yum yum?

AVERY.   I have a date.

MICHAEL.   Do you?

AVERY. A blind date.

MICHAEL. But you're a married woman.

AVERY. Separated.

MICHAEL. Is he a doctor? I think it's always a good idea to marry a doctor don't you? Such a stable and secure life.

AVERY. They say doctors are the most likely to fool around. Followed by cops.

MICHAEL. Cops too? That's too bad. That was my next suggestion. Find yourself a cop. One with a mustache. That meaty beefy kind of man with a mustache. That's what you need.

AVERY. Order if you're gonna order.

MICHAEL. I don't want to keep you from your mystery date.

AVERY. I'll order for you.

MICHAEL. You'll *order* for me?

AVERY. Dear Abby says you shouldn't give a bum money, you should take him to the nearest restaurant and order him some food.

MICHAEL. But what he wants is a drink.

AVERY. Exactly.

MICHAEL. What kind of gift is that? What kind of ... Dear Abby leaves the restaurant feeling terrific but I swear to you that bum, incidentally we don't call them bums anymore, that sobriety-challenged person, resents the imposition on his valuable time. In the time it takes to order and eat that Blue Plate Special he could have hustled enough quarters for a bottle of tequila and be nearing a delicious dinner of worm.

AVERY. I can't do this. I just can't do this. You don't even seem to *want* to stop. You're not working, you don't care about working....

MICHAEL. How can I work? How can I even think about working? All I can think about is you, the lack of you.

AVERY. It's not that I *want* a divorce....

MICHAEL. Divorce? Then why did you say it?

AVERY. But I can't be with you when you're this far gone.

MICHAEL. You're not with me. That's the whole problem.

AVERY. It's not the whole problem. I can't live in this limbo, I need some kind of ... clarity. If not progress, then, at least, an ending.

MICHAEL. I haven't had a drink tonight. Did you notice that? When you're with me, it's like I don't even need to....
AVERY. If you loved me you'd stop.
MICHAEL. Come with me to the meeting and I can. I will.
AVERY. When is the meeting?
MICHAEL. I don't know. We have to call the number.
AVERY. You haven't even called. Good-bye Michael.
MICHAEL. Just give me another chance, I'll play dead, I'll roll over, I'll jump through fire.... *(Michael lights a lighter and makes two legs with his fingers. They jump through the flames while Michael hums circus music then finishes by making a canned applause sound effect.)* And now it's time for Salt and Pepper Theater! Mod Squad! *(He takes two salt shakers and a pepper. He makes them run while singing something like the Mod Squad theme song,* then one of the salt shakers falls.)* "Julie!" Porgy and Bess. *(He takes two pepper shakers and hums.)* The Kennedy Assassination. *(He takes two salt shakers. Makes gun noise. One salt shaker falls and spills. Avery laughs sharply.)* You know a lot of people think the Kennedy assassination isn't funny. *(Avery's laughter turns slightly hysterical then turns to tears.)*

BLACKOUT

Scene 2

A Japanese restaurant. Greed.

DATE. Let's face it, in the old days, and I'm talking not so very long ago, a wife was a liability. I'm not talking emotionally, of course. I'm talking financially. Fiscally speaking.
AVERY. On the other hand.
DATE. Here we go....
AVERY. They worked for free. They cooked. They cleaned.
DATE. You're a feminist.
AVERY. Just in the sense....

* See Special Note on Songs and Recordings on copyright page.

DATE.   Uh-huh.

AVERY.   I think women should be paid the same for the same work.

DATE.   *If* it's the *same* work.

AVERY.   Of course.

DATE.   I mean, a moving man, this is just an example, a moving man can lift, what 200 pounds a load? A woman can lift half that. She should get half his hourly wage, right?

AVERY.   Well....

DATE.   The *same* pay for the *same* work, isn't that what you said?

AVERY.   What if she works harder?

DATE.   Twice as hard?

AVERY.   Yes.

DATE.   Then they should get the same wage. So. You have a job or something?

AVERY.   Yes I'm a traffic watcher. An aerial traffic reporter. I know it doesn't *sound* like much....

DATE.   Hey, it doesn't matter what it *sounds* like....

AVERY.   But it's important in its way, I mean people are trying to get to work and to get home, and they're looking to me to tell them which roads to take, and because I can see more than they can, I know more than they do and I tell them what I know, and because of that, they can, whatever, make it to their kid's softball game on time.

DATE.   It pays well?

AVERY.   Enough.

DATE.   What's enough?

AVERY.   You want to know how much I make?

DATE.   No, I'm just saying, hypothetically, philosophically, what is enough? Answer: enough is enough.

AVERY.   Right.

DATE.   You like your, uh....

AVERY.   Salmon.

DATE.   You like it?

AVERY.   It's a little dry.

DATE.   Waiter!

AVERY.   I'll eat it.

DATE.   If you're not happy with your fish, send it back. It's your money. Well actually, it's my money.

AVERY.   It's my fish.

DATE.   Fair enough.

AVERY.   So Jonathan....

DATE.   Jon. Please. Please.

AVERY.   So, John....

DATE.   When somebody calls me Jonathan I feel like they're talking to somebody else.

AVERY.   So, John....

DATE.   That's J-O-N without the "h"....

AVERY.   What do you do?

DATE.   Do? I've got a lot of irons in the fire right now. A number of investment opportunities. Can you keep a secret?

AVERY.   Yes.

DATE.   Siberian beer.

AVERY.   I've heard of that.

DATE.   You can't have. It doesn't exist. *Yet.*

AVERY.   Oh.

DATE.   The world is changing.

AVERY.   Maybe.

DATE.   Definitely. The walls of Jericho are tumbling down. When I say Siberia what do you think of?

AVERY.   Work-camps?

DATE.   No you don't. You think cold.

AVERY.   I guess.

DATE.   Siberia is cold. And how do you like your beer?

AVERY.   Cold.

DATE.   They're in a hell of a mess over there. People will work for nothing. I'm opening a brewery. I got a designer working on the label as we speak. First he says hammer and sickle, I say uh-uh, communism has bit the big one, deservedly so I might add. I say, let's use a..., you know what I'm gonna say?

AVERY.   A sleigh?

DATE.   On a beer label?

AVERY.   Well.

DATE.   A *bear*. Russia. All that. A bear in a bearskin hat.

AVERY. That's sort of weird.

DATE. Weird?

AVERY. It's sort of cannibalistic. A bear wearing its own skin.

DATE. Let me tell you something. In every animal group, there's a cannibal. A hawk eats baby birds right out of the nest. Killer whales chomp on other whales.

AVERY. Do bears eat other bears?

DATE. No, they eat fish and stuff.

AVERY. Then why would it be wearing its own skin?

DATE. It's wearing a *hat.*

AVERY. I know but it's a bearskin hat.

DATE. It's what they wear in Russia.

AVERY. It's what bears wear?

DATE. No. *Russians.* It's like ... playful.

AVERY. Oh.

DATE. I mean it's a beer label, not an encyclopedia entry.

AVERY. So you're an entrepreneur?

DATE. Well I'm wearing a lot of hats these days, but I'm loving it ... mind you, I'm not as liquid as I could be, my mortgage is killing me, but it's what I wanted. I said to the real estate guy, I want to be pushed to the max of my income potential, and the house is evaluating like crazy. I may be broke but I'm getting rich.

AVERY. Where's your house?

DATE. Eureka Valley.

AVERY. The Castro?

DATE. I know what you're thinking.

AVERY. I'm not thinking that.

DATE. It was Eureka Valley long before the gays moved in. It was the best value for the money. Lots of available real estate there right now. I'm not saying "thank God they're dying so there's real estate opportunities in Eureka Valley," I'm not saying that at all. I'm saying it's an act of God. What, I should not buy a house when there's bargains to be had? Who's that gonna help?

AVERY. No one.

DATE. It's not that I don't feel sorry. I mean, I walk to the grocery, I pass these ghost people. They're so thin you can look right through them. They're like those fish at the bottom of the ocean.

AVERY.   They're not like fish.

DATE.   Of course they're not like fish, but they're *like* fish, so I mean they're dying, okay, but what can I do?

AVERY.   You could feel sad.

DATE.   I do feel sad, I said I felt sad, but it's not like I ever knew any of them personally.

AVERY.   When you leave a place, is it still there?

DATE.   Is this a trick question?

AVERY.   No.

DATE.   Of course it's still there. What are you driving at?

AVERY.   I just mean, there's something..., you may not know them *personally*, but that doesn't make them any less real. I don't know what I'm saying.

DATE.   I don't know what you're saying either!

AVERY.   I mean, my brother lives there.

DATE.   Oh. How 'bout some dessert?

AVERY.   None for me.

DATE.   You gotta eat.

AVERY.   I have eaten.

DATE.   Hey, this is on me.

AVERY.   I prefer to pay my own way.

DATE.   Fantastic. You girls are fantastic.

AVERY.   So they'll let you open a brewery over there?

DATE.   Hell yeah. And you know who we have to thank for that.

AVERY.   Gorbachev?

DATE.   Mister Reagan. The late, great.

AVERY.   He's not dead.

DATE.   Thank God. Four more years as far as I'm concerned. We never had it so good.

AVERY.   Some people didn't.

DATE.   Some people will never have it good. You know why? 'Cause they don't *believe* they can have it good.

AVERY.   Maybe they're right.

DATE.   They're not right. You've heard of self-made millionaires, haven't you?

AVERY. Yes.

DATE. So any man in this country, I mean any little black kid from wherever could become a millionaire.

AVERY. The odds are against it.

DATE. Hell yeah, the odds are against it. That's the beauty of it ... but let's not get into politics.

AVERY. Why not?

DATE. Sex, politics, religion, you know what they say.

AVERY. What?

DATE. Better not get into them.

AVERY. What else is there?

DATE. Right! Good one. That was a joke, right? You were joking.

AVERY. Sort of. Yes.

DATE. I can't tell.

AVERY. Neither can I.

DATE. Well hell, there's nothing I'd rather talk about than sex.

AVERY. And of course, sex *is* politics. And religion.

DATE. It's my religion! Sex and money. Where there's money can sex be far behind?

AVERY. In this case, yes. *(Beat.)*

DATE. That's a no, right?

AVERY. Right.

DATE. You're one of *those* girls.

AVERY. I'm sorry?

DATE. It's a 80s phenomenon.

AVERY. Is it?

DATE. In my experience. They think taking their time is gonna keep them germ-free.

AVERY. Or jerk-free. *(Beat.)*

DATE. I'll just get the bill. I didn't force you to go out with me. It's a blind date that you said yes to. Why? I suppose it's because women over 30 have as much chance of getting married as being in a terrorist attack. But from what I can see most of you girls would *rather* be taken hostage by a terrorist.

AVERY. I'm 31 years old.

DATE. Doesn't matter to me. You look great.

AVERY.   I'm 31 years old. I'm not a girl.

DATE.   Fine. You're a hag. *(The Date catches a waiter's eye and mimes signing a check.)* I mean, I spend a day at the office, beautiful office, the senior partner, he's a guy with taste. It's Deco this, Deco that, but I'm in a skyscraper with windows that don't open except by accident, like an earthquake. So you got two choices heat or air-conditioning, so all day every day I'm either hot or I'm cold. Today I was cold. I put on my jacket, my nipples are standing on end. I light my lighter and warm my fingertips one by one. I go to the bathroom. I stand near the hand dryer. I hug my computer, to feel the air blowing out the back. Today I was cold, but I was nowhere near as cold as I feel right now sitting next to you. *(Avery looks away.)*

BLACKOUT

Scene 3

Gluttony. Later that night. Helen's apartment. Helen watches TV and eats from an ice cream container. Avery enters, flipping through a stack of mail.

HELEN.   So?

AVERY.   Salmon.

HELEN.   Dessert?

AVERY.   No.

HELEN.   No dessert?

AVERY.   No.

HELEN.   I told you to order dessert. You could have taken a bite and brought the rest home!

AVERY.   I couldn't afford it.

HELEN.   He was paying!

AVERY.   He *was* paying.

HELEN.   He didn't pay?

AVERY.   I paid.

HELEN.   Fucker.

AVERY.   I wanted to pay.

HELEN.   That bad.

AVERY.   He kept speaking Japanese to the waiter who was Latino.

HELEN.   You done with the catalogs? *(Avery hands Helen a stack of catalogs.)*

AVERY.   The mailbox is always stuffed with catalogs.

HELEN.   I know. You order one thing and you're on the list.

AVERY.   I have that address. The one you can write to be taken off.

HELEN.   Why would I want to be taken off? I love catalogs. I used to read books, now I read catalogs. Books are no good. You can't buy anything. Nice suit.

AVERY.   T.J. Maxx.

HELEN.   Looks like Neiman Marcus.

AVERY.   I saw it at Neiman Marcus.

HELEN.   And then you found it at T.J. Maxx?

AVERY.   Yeah.

HELEN.   You were very thrifty. I would have just bought the damn thing at Neiman Marcus.

AVERY.   I can't do that. I just can't do that. Those department stores with the garlands and the glitter and the ... meanwhile the people who work there are working for minimum wage.

HELEN.   They get a discount.

AVERY.   They give them a discount so they can model the store's merchandise, I mean it's not *philanthropic* ... did Michael call?

HELEN.   I don't think so.

AVERY.   You don't *think* so?

HELEN.   There was a hang-up. I was screening.

AVERY.   You should have picked up. Michael won't talk to machines.

HELEN.   I thought you were seeing him tonight.

AVERY.   I did. We met in a bar.

HELEN.   Poor you.

AVERY.   Poor Michael.

HELEN. *Michael's* happy. He's drunk all the time. That's the whole problem. He's fun when he's drunk.

AVERY. I think it would be less fun if you were driving on the freeway and a drunken Michael crashed into you, or if you were his patient and he screwed up your medication, or if you were his wife say....

HELEN. Well I mean of course he's not *fun*....

AVERY. What are you eating?

HELEN. Eaten. Ben and Jerry's. Chunky Monkey.

AVERY. The whole thing?

HELEN. I was sad.

AVERY. Why?

HELEN. I forget.

AVERY. What else did you eat?

HELEN. Excuse me?

AVERY. Forget it.

HELEN. I didn't eat any of your food.

AVERY. No, I know, I....

HELEN. I'm hungry.

AVERY. You said you were sad.

HELEN. That too.

AVERY. Did you have dinner?

HELEN. Sort of.

AVERY. What did you have?

HELEN. Microwave popcorn.

AVERY. Honestly, Helen. They charge you an arm and a leg. Just pop it on the stove.

HELEN. I'm willing to pay for convenience.

AVERY. But they don't even all pop.

HELEN. You have to put it on an upside down plate.

AVERY. Is this the plate you used?

HELEN. Uh-huh.

AVERY. It cracked.

HELEN. It did?

AVERY. You can't put these plates in the microwave. They're *Italian.*

HELEN. I don't know how to cook.

AVERY. Helen, you're 32 years old.

HELEN. Steven used to cook for me.

AVERY. That was five years ago. When do you eat real food?

HELEN. When I go out.

AVERY. You never go out.

HELEN. Well I go out to work....

AVERY. No, you don't! You always say no when the temp agency calls!

HELEN. I don't like strangers!

AVERY. Then why are you temping? *(Beat.)*

HELEN. I guess I should get married or something.

AVERY. Do you want me to make you something?

HELEN. What are you making?

AVERY. What do you want?

HELEN. What do we have?

AVERY. What did you buy?

HELEN. What do you mean?

AVERY. There's a chicken in the freezer. I'll defrost it.

HELEN. That will take hours!

AVERY. I'll do it in the microwave.

HELEN. You can't defrost in the microwave.

AVERY. Of course you can.

HELEN. What setting do you use?

AVERY. Defrost. *(Helen opens a bag of Cheez-Doodles.)* If I make this, will you really eat it?

HELEN. Sure.

AVERY. Then why are you eating that?

HELEN. It's an appetizer.

AVERY. You didn't used to do this.

HELEN. Do what?

AVERY. I mean, you used to take *ballet* classes. You wanted to be a dancer....

HELEN. That was between oceanographer and foreign correspondent. I was 13 years old.

AVERY. You won a spelling bee. Do you remember that? You had your picture in the paper.

HELEN. Hey, we all have our 15 minutes....

AVERY.   Nobody I work with knows how to spell, but you know how to spell, I mean you're *smart,* but you just sit in this apartment day after day watching television and reading catalogs....

HELEN.   You're smart too, but where has it gotten you? You're like the traffic girl at some dopey radio station....

AVERY.   Well at least I'm not slumped in a bean bag chair, wearing sweat pants and eating Chee-tos....

HELEN.   Being smart doesn't mean anything, it may even hurt, particularly if you're a woman....

AVERY.   That's just ... I mean maybe you'd like to go around the corner to the group home, and tell the mentally-retarded people they should be grateful because a high I.Q. is really just a *burden....*

HELEN.   Now I'm insensitive to retards?!

AVERY.   *Retards!?*

HELEN.   It was a joke!

AVERY.   I don't find any of this funny. You're just wasting your life. I mean it's like coming home to some trailer park where everyone's on welfare and nobody sees a way out....

HELEN.   Jesus, Avery! I'm not Elvis in the final years! So I had a pint of ice-cream! So I'm eating some Chee-tos!

AVERY.   Fine. Eat Chee-tos. I'm tired of trying to help you. But you're getting fat and I know you know because those are the only things in your closet that still fit. And I think you should know, there's a smell Helen, and when you walk into this apartment, it hits you like a wall, and it's a mixture of all the popcorn and the souvlaki and the dumplings and it's disgusting! Sometimes I have to hold my nose! Sometimes I can't even *look* at you! Your face is like anthropomorphizing into this giant pig! *(Beat.)*

HELEN.   Gee, it's nice to have you home Avery.

AVERY.   Anthropomorphizing is actually when you ascribe human qualities to an animal, so that was the wrong word. That really didn't make any sense.

HELEN.   What you meant was my face is changing into this giant pig face.

AVERY. Well ... yes.

HELEN. But you had to use the big word, even if it was wrong.

AVERY. Well I was only using the big word because I thought it was right. More right. More exact.

HELEN. And of course a bigger word would make me feel smaller.

AVERY. I'm not trying to make you feel small, I'm trying to help you!

HELEN. Uh-huh.

AVERY. I am! But maybe what you really need is....

HELEN. What?

AVERY. Professional help.

HELEN. Oh? Why?

AVERY. Well a professional could be more detached....

HELEN. More detached than you? God help me.

AVERY. I'm not detached! *(Helen snorts.)* I'm not! I just hate....

HELEN. What? What do you hate?

AVERY. Nothing.

HELEN. You hate me.

AVERY. I don't hate you!

HELEN. You hate everybody.

AVERY. Helen.... *(But Helen turns up the television. Eats a handful of Chee-tos. Avery exits.)*

BLACKOUT

Scene 4

Envy. The next day. The helicopter.

FRED. Jason Ludlow? News Director? Ludlow? News Director? He doesn't even have a liberal arts degree, he has some lame-o degree in communications while *I* have a B.A. from a very good school, top of my class, *summa* or *magna* or *cum*

27

laude anyway, and I'm flying a helicopter and he's promoted to News Director.

AVERY.   I thought you liked flying!

FRED.   Six-year-old boys like flying! I want to boss, I want to manage, I want to administrate ... he couldn't administrate himself out of paper bag! He's a hothead, he's a maniac, he's like a serial killer without the van! He's good looking all right, he's good looking, but this is radio! I ask you. Do you think someone can sound good looking?

AVERY.   It's when they try to sound good looking that it's hopeless....

FRED.   Exactly, you're exactly right, and that is just what he does, he *tries* to sound good looking and the result is, well frankly, the result is smarmy. You shouldn't deliver the news in some sort of smoldering bedroom voice, do you think?

AVERY.   Not on this station....

FRED.   No, exactly, you're exactly right, it's inappropriate for this *kind* of station, maybe if we were some sort of loosey-goosey FM alternative rock station, but this is news and this is the weather my friend, traffic reports, stock reports, barometer rising, falling, our listeners know what a barometer is and what it means when it does what it does, we're catering to the busy executive, the man who wants his news and he wants it now....

AVERY.   Or woman....

FRED.   Or woman, exactly, or woman, and it's insulting to her, our female listener to have this smarmy bedroom cunt-sucking voice creaming over the radio. It's sexist that's what it is, it's offensive....

AVERY.   You're taking this promotion too personally, you're interpreting it as a slap in the face....

FRED.   It is a slap in the face! I've been here nine years, this guy waltzes in, and suddenly I'm Oedipus! Banished! To roam the Bay Area! Maybe if I had spent my lunch hours at the Armani boutique....

AVERY.   So he dressed for success....

FRED.   Dress for success! I can't afford to dress for success! Maybe if I had some success I could dress for success! Dress for success! How shallow, how surface, how … have you seen his *socks?*

AVERY.   Frankly, I've got better things to think about than socks.

FRED.   You haven't, if you had, you'd remember 'em, they always have little things on them, little champagne glasses on New Year's Eve, little golf clubs, little ducks, little dice, they're brightly colored, it's like jacket, pants, SOCKS, shoes. God only knows what he spends on those socks, he's spending my raise on his socks, I go to Johnson, I want a raise, he goes "there's no money'," then how can that guy afford those socks!

AVERY.   What do you need a raise for?

FRED.   What do I … for my self-respect, Jesus Christ, is that too much to ask, you hate your job they should pay you more! I got expenses, I got things that break, I got the IRS charging me 67 cents a day interest, I got two kids need braces, I got a car that goes through the oil, in San Francisco, you pay to pee, not to mention the earthquakes.…

AVERY.   There were tremors yesterday.

FRED.   Not in his office. His office is on bedrock. His office is the size of the Coliseum in Rome, his office has an echo, there's no office for Fred but.…

AVERY.   What do you need an office for? You're in the air.

FRED.   I'm a grown man. I need an office. I bring my kids to work, what do they see? A little cubicle, a little carpet partition they post bullshit memos on, like don't sit on the Xerox machine and Xerox your butt!

AVERY.   Why not?

FRED.   I don't know, it's something about the oils in the skin.

AVERY.   Who sat on the Xerox machine?

FRED.   Who knows?!

AVERY.   If you really want to get promoted you should stop acting like the world is kicking your chair, quit bitching, be cheerful.

FRED.   Little Mary Sunshine over here, on the rag at every station meeting about the evils of Styrofoam and the glass ceiling and how come the secretaries' mailboxes are listed by their first names when we're all listed by our last names! You know why? 'Cause nobody knows their last names! It's no big mystery, it's no big conspiracy, it's no big sexist, classist, plot!

AVERY.   Well at least I know enough to be civil to my boss....

FRED.   And where has it gotten you? Scribbling on a clipboard and choking on exhaust fumes....

AVERY.   Well I don't plan to be a Traffic Watcher forever ...

FRED.   Like me, you mean?

AVERY.   I didn't say that....

FRED.   You're just slumming, biding your time, treading water, until the day I'm just a chapter in the great broadcaster's memoir, a little local color, a pathetic little knew-you-when who spent nine pathetic years....

AVERY.   What's pathetic is not knowing that there's more to life than some stupid job....

FRED.   So you think my job is stupid?

AVERY.   Well it's my job too!

FRED.   You're right, it's stupid, it's idiotic, who'd miss us? *(Fred turns the helicopter around.)*

AVERY.   What are you doing? Where are you going?

FRED.   I want to check out his house.

AVERY.   Whose house?

FRED.   Ludlow's.

AVERY.   You're not serious.

FRED.   It'll just take a second.

AVERY.   We're supposed to be covering the bridge!

FRED.   Yeah yeah yeah.

AVERY.   It's? 7:48!

FRED.   We've got seven minutes. Relax. There's more to life than jobs.

AVERY.   They're gonna see that we used extra gas.

FRED.   We're almost there. It's a hop, skip and a jump.

AVERY.   You're obsessing.

FRED.   I'm not obsessing.

AVERY.   It isn't healthy.

FRED.   What are you my shrink?

AVERY.   Look, let's just go to the bridge, do the report and then we can come back.

FRED. I have to know.

AVERY. Why?

FRED. I have a right to know.

AVERY. This is insane.

FRED. There it is! There it is! Look, look look. Is that a lap pool?

AVERY. It's a drainage ditch....

FRED. Fuck me! It's a lap pool! Look in the driveway, look in the driveway, it's a Porsche, when did this guy win the lottery?

AVERY. That's not his car.

FRED. A hot tub! A hot tub!

AVERY. Fred, stop hovering! They see us, everybody sees us, they're all coming out of their houses....

FRED. Oh my God! There she is! How come that asshole gets to come home to that?

AVERY. Go go go go, she's gonna see the call letters....

FRED. What, we're checking on the traffic....

AVERY. There's no traffic in the Oakland hills. She's gonna tell Jason....

FRED. What's he gonna do? Fire me?

AVERY. Please Fred, please, please, please ... this thing with Jason....

FRED. You wouldn't understand. It's a man thing.

AVERY. He got a promotion you wanted.

FRED. Oh you think that's what this is all about?

AVERY. Well ... yes.

FRED. Well you're dead wrong, you couldn't be more wrong, that is way off base.

AVERY. Is my watch right? It hasn't changed! *(They both hear the cue in their headsets.)*

FRED. Shit. It's 7:55 and we're live on high with the bridge report ... over to you Avery.

BLACKOUT

31

Scene 5

The News Director's office. Wrath.

JASON.   A cattle truck tips over on the Oakland Bridge, state troopers are lassoing *steers,* there's piles of *cowshit* in every lane, traffic is backed up to Santa Cruz and you tell them to *take* the Bridge....

AVERY.   Well we didn't actually tell them to *take* it....

JASON.   You said, and I quote, "bridge traffic moving nicely, things are humming along!" To me traffic at a standstill doesn't hum, it doesn't sing, it doesn't have an aria, did you mean the traffic is *honking* along, or perhaps you meant *mooing,* that the traffic was *mooing* along, because the cows were moving along nicely, they were moving along so nicely they had to bring in zoo keepers with tranquilizer guns to get the damn cattle back on the truck! *(Collects himself.)* A pregnant woman gave birth in a car, she literally gave birth in the backseat of a car in the middle of a stampede because you told her husband to take the bridge....

AVERY.   Is that true?

JASON.   Look at my phone messages, look at my little pink things! People are threatening to sue, they're threatening....

AVERY.   We screwed up....

JASON.   Tell me something I don't know! I'm asking for some kind of explanation, I want to understand how all this shit can be going on, and you don't *see* it, or why you might see it and opt *not* to cover it?

AVERY.   Well we covered it on the 8:55....

JASON.   Who gives a shit about the 8:55, anybody who's anybody is at work by 8:55! Where the hell were you at 7:55?!

AVERY.   Well we got a little behind schedule....

JASON.   Doing what?! Who the hell was piloting?

AVERY.   Well, it doesn't really matter who was piloting....

JASON.   I require your loyalty, Avery and more than that, I deserve your loyalty, but maybe you're uncomfortable with the new regime?

AVERY. Jason, you're the News Director, you're not Castro....

JASON. Like my wife, you belittle me. She, we're working on this, but she undermines my maleness, my power....

AVERY. I am not uncomfortable with you being News Director....

JASON. Loyalty! Is that too much to ask?

AVERY. I don't understand what you're asking of me....

JASON. Where were you at 7:55?

AVERY. We were in the Oakland Hills.

JASON. There's no traffic in the Oakland Hills!

AVERY. Well you never know....

JASON. But I do know, I live in the Oakland Hills....

AVERY. You live in the Oakland Hills?

JASON. Is that on your route? Has that ever been on your route?

AVERY. Well no, but....

JASON. Then why the hell were you in the Oakland Hills?!

AVERY. We wanted to see your house.

JASON. What the fuck?!

AVERY. We just wanted to see your house....

JASON. *You* wanted to see my house?

AVERY. Just on a lark....

JASON. Or did Fred want to see my house?

AVERY. Well I don't remember whose idea it was....

JASON. *Try.*

AVERY. We just got to talking and....

JASON. Avery! Try harder.

AVERY. He said it was a man thing.

JASON. Was there a car in the driveway?

AVERY. Yes....

JASON. Did he see it?

AVERY. Who? Fred?

JASON. What kind of car was it?

AVERY. A Porsche I think....

JASON. That's it. He's gone. And *you're* letting him go.

AVERY. I can't fire Fred!

JASON. Don't say "can't" to me! I banish the word!

AVERY.   He's been here longer than any of us....

JASON.   I can't have it! I can't have him gloating at the water cooler, telling every secretary and Xerox repairman....

AVERY.   Telling them what?

JASON.   My wife is having an affair.

AVERY.   Don't tell me this.

JASON.   She smells of sex.

AVERY.   Oh God.

JASON.   Does he know?

AVERY.   Who?

JASON.   You know who.

AVERY.   Fred? No! How would he know? It was just a car in the driveway.

JASON.   You're lying!

AVERY.   Look, I think the two of you need to sit down and....

JASON.   I don't like meetings and memos and personnel reports, somebody challenges me I want to meet them on the battlefield, on the mat, on the briny. I was almost fired for punching a man!

AVERY.   You can't just embark on some reign of terror!

JASON.   I have muscles. Big muscles. Coiled springs, storehouses of energy. Sometimes I strike out like a snake! Better you should tell him.

AVERY.   That's not my job!

JASON.   I banish the words!

AVERY.   You can't just keep banishing the words I happen to say to you!

JASON.   Did you ever have an affair?

AVERY.   I'm separated.

JASON.   But when you were together.

AVERY.   This is ... inappropriate. (*Jason suddenly bolts from behind the desk and squeezes into Avery's chair beside her.*)

JASON.   Do you like me?

AVERY.   Jason....

JASON.   My wife doesn't seem to ... like me. Is there something about me that makes you hunger for other men? If I was on top of you would you be fantasizing about somebody

playing in the Davis Cup? *(Avery stands up, horrified.)*
AVERY.   What?
JASON.   The television's been on for days. She's been watching since the *first round!*
AVERY.   Who is she watching?
JASON.   All of them. It's the shorts, it's the strokes, it's the … not-me-ness of it.
AVERY.   He must play tennis.
JASON.   What?
AVERY.   This sudden interest.
JASON.   Of course!
AVERY.   Maybe the two of you should get some counseling.
JASON.   *(Laughing.)* Yeah right Miss Marital Advice who happens to be separated! *(Jason returns to his desk. Avery pursues him.)*
AVERY.   I don't think that I should have to fire Fred.
JASON.   So you've said. I respect your counsel and I choose to ignore it.
AVERY.   I just think … he's a good traffic watcher.
JASON.   What's a bad traffic watcher?
AVERY.   He knows all the roads.
JASON.   He's got a *map!*
AVERY.   Look. Somehow Fred had it in his head that *he* was getting the promotion and he just needs some time to digest the fact that....
JASON.   A *promotion?*
AVERY.   He's been here nine years!
JASON.   Nobody else would have him!
AVERY.   He's extremely loyal to the station....
JASON.   I am the station! *Le* station *c'est moi!*
AVERY.   If I were you I'd show him a little respect....
JASON.   If you were me?
AVERY.   Give him a raise, throw him a bone....
JASON.   Oh, you think you're management material, okay, then make a managerial decision. The bottom line is the axe has got to fall, one of the morning traffic watchers has got to go … now who's it gonna be? You or Fred?
AVERY.   I never said I was management material!

JASON.   Oh come on, Avery, every day you put seventy-nine notes in the suggestion box, we should do this, we should do that, we should bring our own mugs, we should Xerox on both sides of the page....

AVERY.   I can't make a decision like that! I can't finger a co-worker! I mean this isn't *Rumania* ... *(Jason holds up his hand. Avery stops talking.)*

JASON.   I don't want to pull rank. I don't enjoy pulling rank.

AVERY.   No.

JASON.   But you said, and I quote, "not my job." *That* is not the kind of can-do attitude I'm looking for in my employees. I think we're coming up against the team player problem. Are you a team player, Avery?

AVERY.   Yes.

JASON.   Have you ever *played* on a team?

AVERY.   Of course.

JASON.   A *varsity* team?

AVERY.   I do aerobics.

JASON.   Bingo. Each gal bouncing up and down on her own.

AVERY.   We follow a leader.

JASON.   But you don't work together, do you. You've never had the experience of working *with* someone....

AVERY.   I work with Fred....

JASON.   Which is why *you* should fire him.

BLACKOUT

Scene 6

Pride. A hospital room. Gerard in bed.

AVERY.   I brought you magazines.

GERARD.   Magazines! Yay!

AVERY.   Some of them got a little wet.

GERARD.   Wet magazines. Boo.

AVERY.   They're not wet anymore. But they buckled.

GERARD.   The crowd doesn't know how to respond to buckled. There aren't any famous people in those magazines, are there?

AVERY.   What kind of famous people?

GERARD.   Famous people that are younger than me.

AVERY.   Don't read *Interview.*

GERARD.   How bad is it?

AVERY.   The oldest one is 22. *(Gerard shrieks in horror, it becomes a coughing fit. Avery brings him a glass of water.)* They're all related to someone. They're like daughters of producers or younger brothers of famous actors.

GERARD.   I've been reading the Portland *Herald.* Look at the obituaries. Frank Lannagan, 78, feed salesman. Dorothea Bowdoin, 82, piano teacher. They all die at the right age and they're all nobodies. It's much less depressing than reading the New York *Times.* You won't forget? *(Avery shakes her head no.)* You have to *pressure* them.

AVERY.   I will.

GERARD.   'Cause if the obit doesn't go in within three days it's no longer news. A person dies is news. A person *stays* dead is not. Oh, oh, oh, and I left out a credit, a STREETS OF SAN FRANCISCO credit. You'll insert it?

AVERY.   Of course.

GERARD.   Or do you think they'll turn up their nose at television? What do I care? I'm dead. Nice jacket.

AVERY.   T.J. Maxx.

GERARD.   T.J. Maxx! I miss T.J. Maxx. The max for the minimum. Did I tell you about the Armani I found there? "Only about a million times Gerard" I'm becoming a deathbed bore. I never go out. I have no new stories to tell. Except, oh my God, this doctor, he's an intern, Manuel, gorgeous, and gay, or bi anyway, he gives me something to cover my sores for! Pick up some more of that stuff Marla Hanson sells, okay?

AVERY.   Sure.

GERARD.   How do I look? Do I look all right?

AVERY.   Well to me, you always....

GERARD.   No, I don't mean you, I mean of course to you,

you're my sister, you know the inner me blah blah blah, to *him,* an objective bisexual intern....

AVERY.   Well I'm sure he's seen AIDS patients before....

GERARD.   Obviously. This is San Francisco....

AVERY.   So I mean, I'm sure he factors all that in....

GERARD.   So the answer is beautiful for an AIDS patient?

AVERY.   Well you look sick, Gerard, I mean not sick, but thin.

GERARD.   So the answer is no longer beautiful?

AVERY.   I didn't say that.

GERARD.   *(Flipping through magazines.)* Well I think I look beautiful. I think I have a certain consumptive charisma. Do you know they used to believe that consumptives came back from the dead to steal the life from the living? This is like New England, right? Our forefathers reopened graves and mutilated the corpses, they burned the remaining skin and crossed the tibula, fibula, what do you call the leg bones, in front of the chest and removed the corpses' heads. I do think that's a bit much, don't you? You'll see to it that none of that goes on, right? Whatever you do, *don't* donate my body to science, my God, these doctors, I know what they do to cadavers, it's all one big ha-ha, gallows humor, who can make the biggest gross-out joke.... They'd be standing there looking at my body, without a clue, without an *inkling* that in my time men *threw* themselves at me, that *poems* were written about me, well okay maybe not written, but certainly copied out of books and *sent* to me, and that my memory is being carried around the Castro in endless ... do you think he's worried he might get fired if he has an affair with me?

AVERY.   Well I think he's probably worried he might get AIDS....

GERARD.   Oh there's plenty of things we could do without exchanging bodily fluids. I mean we could *talk,* that was always my favorite part, when did you first notice me, what was your first sexual fantasy about me, when did you first realize you had it bad....

AVERY.   Well maybe a hospital isn't conducive to that kind of....

GERARD.   Not conducive? Look at me, I'm all a twitter!

AVERY.   Did you feel that? The earth moved.

GERARD.   Did I ever.

AVERY.   They say a big one's coming.

GERARD.   Good, if everyone dies I won't feel so put upon.

AVERY.   No really, did you feel it?

GERARD.   Of course I felt it. It was a tremor. I was just trying to enjoy the vibration, it's as close to orgasm as I get these days.

AVERY.   I talked to Mom last night.

GERARD.   Oh?

AVERY.   She sent her love.

GERARD.   She could send her love more directly.

AVERY.   She doesn't like to call the room. She's always worried she's gonna wake you up. She thinks you need your sleep.

GERARD.   I'll have most of eternity to catch up on my sleep.

AVERY.   Well you could always call her....

GERARD.   Can we talk about something else?

AVERY.   Look at your beautiful flowers, who brought them?

GERARD.   The nurse. Somebody died down the hall. I hate flowers, don't ever send me flowers, lilies are the worst, disgusting flower, the Pre-Raphaelites can have them as far as I'm concerned....

AVERY.   Who sent you lilies?

GERARD.   I can't remember, I can't keep them all straight, what with all the flowers and the cards, you know Get Well cards no longer apply, what we really need is an "I'm Sorry You're Dying" card, the numbers are out there, the market is wide open....

AVERY.   So you've been having a lot of visitors?

GERARD.   Tons, oodles, heaps o' visitors.... *(Pointing to magazine.)* Look at this, that's fashion? I could do better than that at the Salvation Army, I *did* do better than that at the Salvation Army.... Do you think he's handsome? Honestly, do you think he's handsome?

AVERY.   He's sort of blah....

GERARD.   He looks like a big faggot, doesn't he look like a big faggot? That lumberjack shirt isn't fooling anyone. *I* could have been a model....

AVERY.   I thought you did do some modeling....

GERARD.   That was just an insurance brochure, a *health* insurance brochure as a matter of fact, which is sort of a ha-ha when you think about it, when you look at me now, breaking the bank....

AVERY.   Is your insurance covering everything?

GERARD.   What do I care? Bill away, I'll be dead.

AVERY.   But Mom and Dad might have to....

GERARD.   I'm not gonna walk out on the check, if that's what you're worried about....

AVERY.   They want to see you.

GERARD.   What are they gonna do? Come and bore me to death? They'll mess up the whole deathbed scene, they'll say I told you so and wear leisure suits.

AVERY.   Does it really matter what they wear?

GERARD.   Yes it does matter as a matter of fact, style is very important to me, style is the expression of everything that you are and I do not want to spend my last days on Earth with people who are essentially polyester. It's not that hard to look good for heaven's sake, just look at the people who know how to dress and copy them, just learn which are the good fabrics and *buy* them. Honestly if people would just shell out a little more for their clothes the world would be a better place. Which reminds me, I want to be buried in the aforementioned Armani, the cream not the navy, or do you think it's too late in the season for cream? I bought the navy because it was more slimming, ha-ha. When I *think* of the time I wasted dieting. Now I could eat anything in the world I want and I'm not hungry anymore. That's like some kind of what? What's that like?

AVERY.   A cautionary tale?

GERARD.   A fairy tale! *(Gerard laughs at his own joke.)*

AVERY.   They wouldn't be here long. Just a weekend. And by the time Dad finds a parking place it will be time to go home.

GERARD. The last time Mom came she took more naps than I did. When people ask what my childhood was like, I tell them to read *The Legend of Sleepy Hollow*.

AVERY. Gerard, they may not have another chance to see you....

GERARD. There's just too many people to deal with right now.

AVERY. Did your volunteer come today?

GERARD. My "AIDS buddy?"

AVERY. What's his name?

GERARD. His name *was* Timmy. I fired him.

AVERY. Why?

GERARD. He was boring.

AVERY. Well Gerard, he wasn't a clown that you hire out for parties....

GERARD. He kept giving me these earnest, pitying looks.... *(He mock shudders.)* Bleeh.

AVERY. He was supposed to help you....

GERARD. With what?

AVERY. With insurance, with landlords, whatever....

GERARD. I don't see why I should hang out with someone I would never have hung out with when I was well. I hate those little guys who bulk up to compensate for their height and end up looking like *mailboxes*. And he stood too close, he had bad breath and he was *nervous,* I swear to God, I'd ask him to pass me the newspaper, and he'd mentally use *tongs,* I'd sneeze and the guy would nearly do a Dick Van Dyke running to open the window....

AVERY. Oh Gerard, they train these people, I'm sure he knows better than that....

GERARD. Anyway, he was flirting with Manuel, I *saw* them in the hallway, it's like I'm out of the running, I'm somebody's maiden aunt, or a little boy sent to bed without his supper, I mean HELLO? I'M STILL HERE!

AVERY. Well I thought he seemed nice.

GERARD. Well I always liked Michael but you got rid of him.

AVERY. Michael is hopeless. He doesn't eat, he doesn't work,

41

he's....

GERARD.   Slothful?

AVERY.   I haven't heard that word for years.

GERARD.   The opposite of slothful is anal, and that's no day at the beach either ... remember when your *Seventeen* would come in the mail and you wouldn't even let me flip through it before you'd read it, you didn't want me to break the binding....

AVERY.   Mom and Dad are coming next weekend.

GERARD.   Oh, Avery I told you I don't want to deal with them....

AVERY.   There was a fare war! They bought a ticket!

GERARD.   Well, I guess now I have to hurry up and die....

AVERY.   Why do you have to be so mean?

GERARD.   You didn't go through it with Mom and Dad, you weren't there, you were romping through the Ivy when the shit hit the fan....

AVERY.   It was an adjustment for them and you couldn't expect them to....

GERARD.   I expected them to love me....

AVERY.   Well you don't make it easy for people to love you, Gerard, you're very hard on people....

GERARD.   Well if that isn't the pot calling the kettle black....

AVERY.   What do you mean by that?

GERARD.   Oh come on Avery, you're up there looking down at us mortals....

AVERY.   You're the one who's been lying there *pronouncing* on....

GERARD.   You're never in the room *with* someone. You're sitting in judgment, deciding whether or not this or that person deserves a piece of you....

AVERY.   You do the same thing....

GERARD.   It's because Mom convinced us that we were better than everyone else ... like she wouldn't let us play with Sukie Edwards because her parents were DIVORCED....

AVERY.   It was a different time....

GERARD.   Or Andy Walters because his father was a TRUCK

DRIVER....

AVERY. It wasn't because he was a truck driver....

GERARD. You're standing there like little Miss Nightingale when all the time you're thinking I'm shallow, I'm careless, I'm promiscuous....

AVERY. Not promiscuous, self-destructive!

GERARD. In your heart of hearts, you can't stop thinking it was my fault I got sick.

AVERY. Well Gerard you slept around....

GERARD. Oh Avery don't....

AVERY. You were so busy trying to prove to yourself that you were attractive that you were going to the baths long after....

GERARD. So this is all my fault?

AVERY. Did you change your behavior after you knew the risks?

GERARD. Well gee Avery, we can't all be perfect like you, we can't all go to Yale where everyone's blonde and lux is *veritas*....

AVERY. I'm not saying I'm perfect....

GERARD. No you don't say very much at all, and what you do say is hurtful, I mean Jesus, couldn't you just tell me I look great? *No,* because that would be a *lie,* that would be a little black mark on your soul, so you cheer me right up by telling me I look like shit....

AVERY. I didn't say you looked like shit....

GERARD. You've got to break a binding when you read a magazine and you've got to get messy when you love someone 'cause there's semen and saliva....

AVERY. That's not love!

GERARD. You've left every man you've ever been involved with....

AVERY. As if you don't go from person to person....

GERARD. I may be a whore but at least I connected!

AVERY. If by connecting you mean having sex....

GERARD. I loved a lot of people and they loved me!

AVERY. And where are they now? Nobody comes to visit you!

GERARD. And who do you have, Avery? Michael? Not anymore! Me? Not for long! You better lower your standards, girl.

Sin a little, it's more fun, it's less lonely. *(The lights flicker as things begin to fall off the bedside table. Sound of earthquake. Avery covers Gerard with her body. The lights go out. A moment later, the emergency lights come up. Sound of car alarms outside.)*
AVERY.   Gerard? *(Gerard's arm falls awkwardly off the bed. A magazine falls.)* Gerard?!

BLACKOUT

INTERMISSION

ACT TWO

Scene 1

The bar. Candlelight. Man at the bar. Avery enters.

MAN. Looking for me?

AVERY. My husband. Have you seen him? The man I was with last night?

MAN. No, but there's been a lot going on. My stool shimmied into the ladies' room.

AVERY. Do you have a car?

MAN. A car? Yes I have a car.

AVERY. Can I borrow it?

MAN. What happened to your car?

AVERY. It got smashed.

MAN. You want the keys to my car? *(He puts his keys on the bar, then stops her with his hand.)* You have to kiss me for them.

AVERY. Are the busses running?

MAN. You got to be kidding. Bridges are bursting open.

AVERY. The Golden Gate?

MAN. Bay.

AVERY. Where did you hear that?

MAN. Why would you take public transportation when a Buick awaits you? When all you have to do is turn this frog into a prince with one little kiss.

AVERY. With tongues?

MAN. Oh yes, tongue. It has to be tongue. *(Avery starts to leave.)*

AVERY. I'll walk.

MAN. I'll drive you.

AVERY. No thanks.

MAN. If I were sober, would you let me drive you home?

AVERY. Probably.

MAN. How about a cup of coffee?

AVERY. That doesn't work.

MAN.   Walk me around. Put an arm around me and walk me around.

AVERY.   I don't have time to get you sober.

MAN.   I'm not sure you'd like me sober anyway. I lose my charm when I'm sober.

AVERY.   Your stool is on my purse.

MAN.   Have you ever been tested? They have a singles club now with cards. Laminated. Renewable. Every month. *(Holds up card.)* See?

AVERY.   Maybe you should try AA instead.

MAN.   I tried that. There were too many steps.

AVERY.   Can you move your stool?

MAN.   I've been tested. I'm negative but I'm a positive kind of guy. Why don't you kiss me? What would it cost you? At the very least it would give me pleasure. At best, it would give us both pleasure. Either way, you'd get the keys to a car. Cruise control. Cassette deck. Rack and pinion steering.

AVERY.   Because that would be prostitution.

MAN.   It might be love.

AVERY.   It's got nothing to do with love. It's lust.

MAN.   What is lust but incipient love?

AVERY.   In this case, love is very unlikely.

MAN.   That hurts my feelings.

AVERY.   I'm sorry.

MAN.   I don't think you really mean that.

AVERY.   I'm sorry about everything bad that's ever happened to you! *(Avery pulls his stool along with the purse.)*

MAN.   Stop! Thief! She's taking my purse!

AVERY.   You have no idea what you're dealing with here, for you it's a snow day, a party, a pick-up ... well maybe another night I could trade kisses for keys and imagine that what you're offering me is love but I have lost more tonight than you could possibly imagine and some sordid make-out session is not gonna ease that pain! *(Beat. Man hands her the purse. Avery starts to exit.)*

MAN.   I saw the guy from last night but he left with a woman.

AVERY.   What woman?

MAN. A pretty woman. Brunette.

AVERY. What were they doing?

MAN. Don't do this to yourself.

AVERY. Why didn't you tell me before?

MAN. I didn't want to hurt you.

AVERY. Right. *(Avery starts to leave.)*

MAN. What does your husband do?

AVERY. He's a doctor.

MAN. That makes sense.

AVERY. Why?

MAN. The woman was dressed in white.

AVERY. Like a nurse? *(Man shrugs.)* Are you sure it was him?

MAN. What does he drink?

AVERY. You tell me.

MAN. Looked like tequila. *(Avery sits.)* People do strange things in a crisis. How 'bout I buy you a drink?

AVERY. I don't want a drink.

MAN. I want to show you a picture. Can I show you a picture?

AVERY. Your wife?

MAN. She was. I gave her that corsage. She saved it. It's in a shoe box in the linen closet. Behind the Desenex.

AVERY. You were going to the prom?

MAN. Sadie Hawkins Dance. She asked me. *She* asked *me*.

AVERY. And then what happened?

MAN. She stopped loving me.

AVERY. Maybe she stopped because you started drinking.

MAN. Maybe she stopped because ... no, other way around. Look at that curl, that one little curl is going the wrong way. And she's standing there smiling. Unaware. I would give anything to go back in time and fix that one little curl.

AVERY. Why don't you go back to her?

MAN. I would give anything to go back but I am condemned to return to bars like this, again and again I chase after the smell of a new shampoo, the infinite promise of the new.... *(Man lifts her hair and lets it fall.)*

AVERY. Do you have a job?

MAN. Why? You want to find out my status? You want to

find out if my points equal yours?

AVERY. What?

MAN. Andy Warhol says that people couple according to a point system. You get a certain number of points for beauty, money, talent, power.... That's why beautiful women and powerful men are so often together, their points are in different categories, but they equal out.

AVERY. That's a depressingly cynical way to look at love.

MAN. Me, I have no money points but that's due to a surfeit of points in the talent category. I'm a poet. If I'd had less talent I'd probably be rich by now.

AVERY. And have you published?

MAN. Now, you're jumping categories. That's not the talent category, that's the success category.

AVERY. They often go together.

MAN. If only that were true.

AVERY. Well have you?

MAN. Yes I have, but you've never heard of me and you've never heard of the magazines because as soon as a magazine publishes one of my poems it goes out of business. *The New Yorker* has been superstitiously rejecting my work for years but of course I've never written a really good garden poem, I've never mastered that sort of change of season wistfulness, and I've never given much thought to squirrels at all.

AVERY. What do you write? Some sort of urban manhole poetry?

MAN. I write love poems as a matter of fact. I write poems about elbows and bellies and lips and how a certain set of those pathetic, chapped, pimpled body parts can break your heart. Tonight I will probably write a poem about you.

AVERY. Before or after we look at your etchings?

MAN. All right, you're an intelligent woman. You know better. But isn't it tempting sometimes to do something you know you'll regret? Look at my hand. Do you know what this hand is? This hand is an instrument of pleasure. Look. I touch my own skin. Nothing. A little warmth, the nerve endings barely rouse themselves but I touch you *(He does.)* and you respond. The nerves jump. You have encountered the other. I find you heartbreakingly beautiful.

AVERY.   I'm not beautiful.

MAN.   You don't let yourself be beautiful.

AVERY.   Why me? Why do you think you want me?

MAN.   Because you're so chilly. It makes me want to find the fire underneath.

AVERY.   Maybe there is no fire.

MAN.   Look me in the eyes and tell me that's true. *(Man kisses her. His hand slides down her ass. Avery breaks away.)*

AVERY.   You didn't see him, did you? Did you?

MAN.   Ladybug, ladybug fly away home, your house is on fire and your husband is home.... *(She runs out of the bar. He watches her leave.)* Now *that's* poetry!

BLACKOUT

Scene 2

The radio station. Ringing phone. Avery enters.

JASON.   Avery, where the hell have you been?

AVERY.   I need to borrow one of the helicopters.

JASON.   You what?

AVERY.   My car got smashed and I've got to get home....

JASON.   *Home?* You want a career tip, Avery? If you work for an all news station, you don't ask for time off during an earthquake. Answer the goddamn phone!

AVERY.   That's not my....

JASON.   And don't you dare tell me that's not your job!

AVERY.   *(Picking up phone.)* KSFB, Hello? The line's dead.

JASON.   Jesus Christ! What did you do?

AVERY.   I didn't do anything. I pressed the button!

JASON.   What button?

AVERY.   The 4700 line.

JASON.   That's what we always press!

AVERY.   I know!

JASON. So what's the problem!

AVERY. Gee I don't know Jason, maybe it has something to do with the *earthquake*....

JASON. You're telling *me* about the earthquake. Believe me I'm aware of the earthquake, I'm aware that it may be the biggest story of my career, but a minute ago, if you can believe this, one of my employees, one of my reporters, came in here asking for time off!

AVERY. Maybe you could get a sub....

JASON. Where's the contact sheet?

AVERY. It's in your hand.

JASON. That's the old contact sheet. Where's the new contact sheet?

AVERY. It's on the computer....

JASON. It's on the *what*?

AVERY. Kathy's doing everything on the computer now....

JASON. Who the hell told her to do that?

AVERY. There was a memo about wasting paper!

JASON. Jesus Christ, save a tree and fuck me.

AVERY. Call information.

JASON. *(Picking up the phone, waiting for the dial tone.)* Why the fuck do people *move*? Do they honestly believe they're gonna be happier in Mill Valley? Jesus Christ, nothing ... do you realize I've got no one in the air?

AVERY. Where's Woody and Jim?

JASON. They're in the blimp! They're at the game! Where's the son-of-a-bitchin' phone book?

AVERY. I'm sure Fred will be in soon.

JASON. I thought I told you to fire Fred.

AVERY. I didn't have the chance.

JASON. Women in the workplace. Want to be everybody's friend!

AVERY. Jason, Fred has a family.

JASON. Have you ever seen them? They're fat. I hate fat people. Kids especially. I hate fat kids. Have you seen the picture on his desk? They barely fit into the frame. And his clothes, Jesus, the polyester blends, and the seams that don't match and the black shoes with the brown pants....

AVERY.   Well nobody *sees* him, he's on the radio.

JASON.   I see him! I'm tired of looking at him. God, I hate poor people. What the fuck am I doing? Get your ass in the air!

AVERY.   Great, I'll just check on my house. And then I'll get right on the air.

JASON.   Wo, wo, wo, wo, I'm sure you *intend* to get on the air, but one thing and another, you get home, things have happened, your Hummel collection has crashed to the floor....

AVERY.   I've never asked for anything, not even a raise, I covered every stupid parade and never got overtime....

JASON.   Your contract is coming up for renewal, isn't it? Maybe it's time to clean house, start fresh, clear out all the dead wood ... a lot of young communications majors out there beating the bushes. Better get out the Oil of Olay. Look what's happening to Jane Pauley.

AVERY.   Oh for God's sake, this is radio.

JASON.   New ideas, new audience....

AVERY.   Nobody gives a shit about the Traffic Watcher....

JASON.   A lot of fine people have spent their careers as aerial traffic reporters, Frances Gary Powers....

AVERY.   He wasn't a reporter, he was a *spy*....

JASON.   But he *died* working as a traffic reporter....

AVERY.   Well believe me, I don't want to die a traffic reporter.

JASON.   You think you're better than that? You're not happy with your job? Maybe you'd be happier on the ground, answering phones, selling ads, 'cause let's face it Avery, you're not much of a journalist —

AVERY.   As if you're a journalist! You're not a journalist, you're a technician, you're like the radio equivalent of a chiropractor! You're this little corporate creature, who runs around with his feathers all puffed up stealing everybody's ideas....

JASON.   I don't believe you ever had an idea worth stealing....

AVERY.   Well it wasn't recognizable by the time you were done with it, women's health care turned into "breast implants, how big should you go...."

JASON. I wouldn't expect you to understand anything about market shares, you don't even have a degree in communications!

AVERY. I went to Yale, where did you go?

JASON. And Yale is certainly known for its journalism program!

AVERY. Eastern Missouri State, I believe?

JASON. Do you have a problem with my credentials?

AVERY. Eastern Missouri State! I hear that's the best journalism program in all of Missouri!...

JASON. Yes I went to Eastern Missouri State and when I got there I bent down and I kissed the ground because I was finally away from my shitbox of a home where my father beat my ass for salting my dinner before he did. I worked in the local bar cleaning up the puke the frat boys left behind and that was after a day of classes and four hours of wrestling practice and sending whatever pathetic money I could home to my little brothers and sisters who grew up to go crazy and take drugs and die in car accidents while I managed to not only stay alive but wear a suit every day. And for that reason when the station owners say jump I say how high. Do you understand what I'm saying to you?

AVERY. Yes.

JASON. Good. Now when I say jump what are you gonna say? I say jump! What are you gonna say to me?

AVERY. All right!

JASON. That is not the answer! That is not the answer! I say jump! What do you say?

AVERY. I'd say Why? I'd want to know why!

JASON. That is not your concern! That is not your concern! I say jump! What do you say?

AVERY. The hell with this....

JASON. And that is why you're 31 years old and still covering traffic tie-ups! Clean out your desk.

AVERY. You're firing me? *(Fred enters.)*

JASON. Where the hell have you been? *(Jason exits. Fred calls after him.)*

FRED. You're welcome!

JASON. *(Reentering.)* What did you just say to me?

FRED. Nothing.

JASON. Did you get any dinner Fred? I hope you got some dinner.

FRED. We were having dinner when....

JASON. What were you having? Meat loaf? Hamburger Helper? Shake n'Bake?

FRED. Just a chicken thing....

JASON. You and the family? How many kids have you got, Fred?

FRED. Three.

JASON. Three? That must cost you an arm and a leg. They must eat you out of house and home.

FRED. Uh-uh.

JASON. And your wife, she works?

FRED. Uh-uh.

JASON. So you're the breadwinner, you bring home the bacon, back to the salt mines, another day, another dollar....

FRED. Uh-huh.

JASON. Is that a new shirt? No, now that I look closer I see that it's fraying around the collar....

FRED. I rushed right over, I didn't have time....

JASON. Where do you buy your shirts?

FRED. My wife buys them. Over the phone I think.

JASON. Over the *phone.* Well they have some first rate catalogs now, of course this doesn't look like it came from one of those, this looks like, let me just look at the tag, 60% polyester, don't you find that hot? I need a shirt to breathe myself, I need a shirt with lungs! *(Jason goes from looking at the tag to twisting the collar tight. Fred tries to speak but only sounds come out.)*

AVERY. For God's sake, Jason, you're strangling him! *(Jason looks sharply at Avery. He slowly realizes what he's doing, shaken, he lets go of Fred's collar.)*

JASON. *(Fixing Fred's shirt.)* Well Fred, it looks like I have to put your sorry ass in the air. *(Jason exits.)*

FRED. *(To Avery.)* How did you get here first? I bust my butt getting over here and you show me up.

AVERY. I wasn't trying to show you up.

FRED. Little Miss Suck-Up, hovering near the office in case catastrophe strikes.

AVERY. I was just trying to borrow a helicopter!

FRED. I never get to borrow a helicopter!

AVERY. At least you have a car. *My* car got smashed.

FRED. By what?

AVERY. A lamp fell on it.

FRED. A *lamp?*

AVERY. A street lamp. A lamp in the hospital parking lot. The cars on either side of me were fine.

FRED. What kind of car was it?

AVERY. Toyota Camry.

FRED. What year?

AVERY. '89.

FRED. A new car?! You drive a new car?

AVERY. I did! I don't now!

FRED. How can you afford a new car? I can't afford a new car!

AVERY. My husband....

FRED. Oh right, the doctor. I got a wife sits on her duff.

AVERY. I've got a husband who's an alcoholic.

FRED. Boo hoo.

AVERY. Can I borrow your car? I have to get home. He may have passed out. There may be a fire.

FRED. And the world may end tomorrow.

AVERY. This is an emergency.

FRED. Oh now it's *your* earthquake.

AVERY. I'm worried about my house, my husband, my cat....

FRED. *Your* cat! Do you realize you never once asked me about *my* cat? *My* house, *my* kids, *my* cat!

AVERY. Are they all right?

FRED. Yes. Thanks for asking. Everyone's fine. Except for the cat. I don't have a cat. I'd *like* to have a cat.

AVERY. Can you lend me your car?

FRED. I'm afraid it'd be a comedown for you.

AVERY. I'll have it back by the time you leave.

FRED. It was really hard to find a parking place.

AVERY.   Where did you park it?

FRED.   In the handicapped space. They get all the good parking places.

AVERY.   You parked it in a handicapped space?

FRED.   As if you never do it!

AVERY.   I don't!

FRED.   Maybe if I had a reserved parking space like Avery Bly on High....

AVERY.   Well I don't have it anymore! I just got fired!

FRED.   You just got fired?

AVERY.   I just got fired!

FRED.   You're leaving me *alone* with him?!

AVERY.   At least you have a job!

FRED.   For now!

AVERY.   I don't know what I'm gonna live on!

FRED.   Alimony! Easy street!

AVERY.   I'm not getting any alimony, we're not even divorced!

FRED.   So get divorced!

AVERY.   I don't want to be divorced, I want to be married, at least you have a family.

FRED.   A fat family! I've heard the snickering, I know my wife is fat, but it's not because she doesn't try! She does the NutraSystem, the Weight Watchers, the Jenny Craig, I'm practically starving ... I mean she was a beautiful woman when I married her, she's beautiful still, I mean not as beautiful as *Jason's* wife but....

AVERY.   Be glad you're not married to Jason's wife....

FRED.   As if Jason's wife is gonna look twice at me....

AVERY.   She might....

FRED.   What?

AVERY.   The car in the driveway....

FRED.   She sleeps around?!

AVERY.   Face it Fred, you've got what he wants, you have a wife who loves you ... who buys you shirts and ... cooks you chicken ... you have children, you have a family!

FRED.   I have what he wants?

AVERY.   Yes!

FRED. You think?

AVERY. I do. You have what *I* want. *(Beat.)*

FRED. Don't lock the doors. The locks are rusted. And ignore the little oil light. It lies.

AVERY. Fred, I owe you.

FRED. Who doesn't?

BLACKOUT

Scene 3

The parking garage. Date is holding a cellular phone to his ear and talking 78 r.p.m.

DATE. An earthquake. California big state. Lots of delegates. Washington concerned. Money comes in. Where is that money going to go? Building supplies, construction companies, heating and cooling. You should be telling me this. Yeah? What's the share?

AVERY. Excuse me?

DATE. Can't you see I'm on the phone? Don't talk to me, talk to them, the price is gonna jump, every goddamn network is here for the Series and you're sitting around with your dick hanging out! Love to Martha. *(Clicks off.)*

AVERY. Do you work in this building? I haven't seen you before.

DATE. You might have seen me before.

AVERY. Oh God.

DATE. You didn't know me before. Not that you know me now. You may think that you know me now.... You may think that because I'm in a certain line of work or wear a certain kind of suit that you know who I am and what I am but you don't.

AVERY. Look, I'm sorry about last night.

DATE. *I'm* sorry about last night. I was looking forward to last night. I bought a new tie.

56

AVERY.   It was a good-looking tie.

DATE.   What did it look like?

AVERY.   I ... can't remember.

DATE.   That doesn't surprise me. I don't believe you ever looked at me. I believe you made up your mind up about me before we even opened the menus.

AVERY.   I probably shouldn't have gone....

DATE.   I asked around for the name of a restaurant, I doodled your name at the office that day, I brought the platinum to impress you, I got there early to get a good table.... I would have done everything in my power to make you happy, if you had only let me, if you had only *smiled,* I would have ... but you thought I had the soul of a businessman.

AVERY.   I never said that....

DATE.   But what's the difference between me and you? I want something, you want something. I want to make money, you want....

AVERY.   To borrow your car. I borrowed a friend's car but it was out of oil.

DATE.   Why on earth should I lend you my car?

AVERY.   Because I need it.

DATE.   I'm a businessman. Need has nothing to do with anything.

AVERY.   I just want to check on my house.

DATE.   You care about your house.

AVERY.   Of course.

DATE.   You care about things.

AVERY.   It's not just my *things....*

DATE.   But you need my thing to check on the things that aren't just things, don't you?

AVERY.   Maybe you could drive me....

DATE.   Oh I'd enjoy that ... we had such a good time together last night. I have a better idea. You want the car? Take it.

AVERY.   You're lending it to me?

DATE.   No.

AVERY.   I don't understand.

DATE.   You want it take it.

AVERY.   Steal it?

DATE.   I'll report it stolen. I'll get the insurance. You'll get the car. Who's going to chase down a stolen car in the middle of an earthquake?

AVERY.   I'm going to return the car....

DATE.   That's not an option, if you steal it you steal it, I could use the cash flow, especially now when there's stock opportunities to be had....

AVERY.   Why don't you just sell the car?

DATE.   You take a loss just by driving it off the lot. I don't care to take a loss....

AVERY.   What did you pay for it?

DATE.   You're gonna *buy* it?

AVERY.   *(Scrambling for her checkbook.)* Yes.

DATE.   I'm sorry we don't take personal checks....

AVERY.   I can afford it. My husband happens to be a doctor....

DATE.   Your *estranged* husband. Forget it.

AVERY.   Why won't you just lend me the car?

DATE.   Why won't you just take the car?

AVERY.   Because, and I know this is a difficult concept for you, because it's wrong.

DATE.   Newsflash ... nobody's watching. There is no God.

AVERY.   This isn't about God, it's about other people. Insurance fraud raises everybody's premiums!

DATE.   Let's see, how much will this one car raise everybody's premiums?

AVERY.   You only see it in terms of yourself, this one car, this one profit....

DATE.   What did I do to become pond scum in your eyes? So I made a little money buying real estate....

AVERY.   At the expense of other people....

DATE.   What other people?

AVERY.   The families of the people with AIDS who sell you their child's house when they're grief-stricken and not thinking straight....

DATE.   Maybe you should walk home.

AVERY.   It's too far! It's in the Marina District.

DATE.   You don't want to go to the Marina District. I hear it's on fire.

AVERY.   Where did you hear that? Is that true?

DATE.   How should I know? You're on the radio.

AVERY.   My house is there, my husband's there...!

DATE.   I'm trying to solve your problem here....

AVERY.   You just want me to sink to your level....

DATE.   But you're never gonna do it, because your candidacy for sainthood is more important to you than your house, your husband....

AVERY.   You don't know me, talking about how I don't know you, feeling sorry for yourself because I don't remember the pattern of your tie, well I've got more important things on my mind, not that I expect you to care but my brother died tonight! *(Beat.)*

DATE.   I had a brother. He died before I was born.

AVERY.   I'm sorry.

DATE.   Why? I never knew him. There were pictures of him everywhere but if my mother even heard his name she'd run into the bedroom and shut the door. One time I came across these boxes of toys in a cellar closet, and I was like great, look at all these toys, and of course they were his and when my mother came down and saw me she like collapsed on the stairs and my father he yelled at me and put a padlock on the closet. Still every time we were in a store and I wanted them to buy me a toy they'd say "but you've got all those toys at home...."

AVERY.   What was his name?

DATE.   His name was Jonathan.

AVERY.   No, *his* name.

DATE.   Jonathan.

AVERY.   But that's your name.

DATE.   Uh-huh.

AVERY.   Oh my God.

DATE.   Listen, if you're looking to unload the property, I might be in a position to make an offer....

AVERY.   What property?

DATE.   Your brother's place.

AVERY.   You sonovabitch. *(Avery snatches the keys and exits. He punches numbers into the telephone.)*
DATE.   Hello, I'd like to report a stolen car.

BLACKOUT

Scene 4

Helen's car. Helen is eating candy bars.

HELEN.   Were you waiting long?
AVERY.   Let's just go.
HELEN.   I stopped everywhere that was open. Just in case. While I was out. Provisions. When the earthquake started, I just kept seeing my body being carried out on a stretcher, I kept seeing my body with a tag on the toe, and my father dialing and dialing trying to get through and it just made me HUNGRY like who gives a damn if I'm fat or I'm thin when I'm a corpse! *(Offering a candy bar.)* You want one?
AVERY.   No thanks, I've got stuff on my hands.
HELEN.   What stuff?
AVERY.   Ink. From the fingerprinting.
HELEN.   Oh my God. Fingerprinting! Did they take your picture? Are you going to be in post offices?
AVERY.   I'm not Wanted. They caught me.
HELEN.   I can't believe it. You've got like a record. You'll have to put it down on job applications. Forever.
AVERY.   Take a left here.
HELEN.   He's not gonna be there.
AVERY.   Get in the right lane.
HELEN.   He's probably out looting liquor stores.
AVERY.   I still want to check on my house.
HELEN.   It's not your house, it's his house.
AVERY.   It's half my house.
HELEN.   You were gonna sell it anyway, that's what you told me.

AVERY.   I just want make sure he's okay.

HELEN.   He's okay, believe me. You and I on the other hand are gonna be caught under an overpass during an after-shock.... Did you have dinner yet?

AVERY.   No, I went straight from work to the hospital.

HELEN.   When was the last time you ate something?

AVERY.   I haven't been very hungry.

HELEN.   You sure you don't want a Nestle's Crunch? I could feed it to you.

AVERY.   No thanks.

HELEN.   You must be hungry.

AVERY.   Even if I were, I wouldn't eat one of those.

HELEN.   Why not? Because it tastes good?

AVERY.   Because it's like eating a giant stick of butter.

HELEN.   *(As if she means it.)* You're so together. You don't drink, you don't eat, you visit people in the hospital, you're perfect.

AVERY.   I'm not perfect.

HELEN.   *(Sharply.)* Well you're not.

AVERY.   I know.

HELEN.   You're so busy being right, you don't care how you make people feel. You make people feel bad. I'm not saying I'm not fucked up, 'cause I know I'm fucked up but you're fucked up and you don't even know it. And there are things, you know, that I haven't mentioned, like you miss the trash can, you know with like your mascara-stained cotton balls, or like you leave the iron plugged in....

AVERY.   I turned it off!

HELEN.   I know but ... *safety,* and you don't erase your messages so I never know if you got them, and like your *shoes* are all over the house wherever they happen to get kicked off and you left a load of laundry in the washer so long it like *mildewed* and I rewashed and dried the entire load using about a million dryer sheets to get the smell out and you never even thanked me....

AVERY.   I didn't know!

HELEN.   And then you imagine you're helping me with your

little Lean Cuisines and broiled chickens without a clue that I just don't care anymore! That I'm fucking tired of trying to look good all the time! Of trying to be thin and young and pretty and tan and toned and sane. Jesus it's all I can do to show up for a job! I mean, you act like I'm some sort of child because I eat ... Chee-tos when the truth is I took you in and took care of you and charged you less than half the rent and listened to about a million Michael stories even though it was fairly obvious that *that* situation was pretty hopeless....

AVERY.   You're one to talk about hopeless situations, you sit there night after night stuffing your face....

HELEN.   We'll see how *you* look after five years of living alone....

AVERY.   I will never get as heavy as you, I don't care what happens to me, nuclear war, I will get my ass to the health club, I will live on spinach greens before I let myself turn into.... You attracted mice, you literally attracted mice with your cartons and your bags and your dips....

HELEN.   I eat when I'm hungry! That's what you're supposed to do!

AVERY.   You don't eat when you're hungry, you don't even know when you're hungry, you eat when you're sad, you eat when you're lonely....

HELEN.   Well whose fault is that? You're never home when you say you're gonna be home....

AVERY.   It's not my fault you sit there and wait for my key in the door! I was trying to take care of a brother and a husband and I'd come home to this giant succubus, this quivering mass of need.... *(Helen screeches to a stop.)* What are you doing? Why did you stop?

HELEN.   We're not going anywhere till you eat a candy bar!

AVERY.   I don't want a candy bar!

HELEN.   Then get out of the car.

AVERY.   You don't mean that.

HELEN.   Oh yes I do.

AVERY.   I can't walk to the Marina District! It's too far!

HELEN.   Hey, it will be really good exercise.

AVERY. Helen, I have to get home.

HELEN. Listen babe, I'm the way home. I got the wheels. And you don't.

AVERY. I'm not hungry!

HELEN. You're a human being and you haven't eaten for a seventeen hours! You're starving!

AVERY. I tell you I'm not.

HELEN. What if I said it would make me happy to see you eat a candy bar?

AVERY. I would say that was insane.

HELEN. Okay, I'm insane. Humor me.

AVERY. I don't feel like humoring you! Helen, my brother died tonight and I just don't feel like eating, I know that's hard for you to understand, but my stomach is so sick and so sad that any food I ate would come right back up. My parents were supposed to come but they didn't come, they were waiting for a better airfare, and I was the only one there and the nurse wouldn't even let me sit with his body. I just wanted to sit with his body, like those Indians on PBS who sat with the body so the soul would have some company on the way to the next world ... but they just *took* him and then right away the stupid nurse stripped the bed like she wanted to erase everything that had ever touched him.

HELEN. Why didn't you tell me Gerard died?

AVERY. I just did.

HELEN. I would never have yelled at you if I'd ... why didn't you tell me?

AVERY. I didn't feel like talking.

HELEN. Why didn't you tell me on the phone?

AVERY. I didn't want to tell you on the *phone.*

HELEN. I can't believe you wouldn't tell me.

AVERY. Now this is about you?

HELEN. I'm your best friend, I'm your oldest friend, I'm maybe your only friend....

AVERY. You're not my only friend.

HELEN. Who are your other friends?

AVERY. I'm not going to list my friends....

63

HELEN.   When my mother died, I came to you. I cried like a baby....

AVERY.   This was different....

HELEN.   How was it different?

AVERY.   We were having a fight when the earthquake hit....

HELEN.   Oh no....

AVERY.   He wanted me to say he was beautiful, he was desperate to hear that he ... I mean he was acting like the hospital was some big sorority house and there were six or seven dream dates waiting downstairs.... You wouldn't believe the petty, petty things coming out of his mouth, models and make-up and television credits ... I just wanted him to have a little dignity, to face up to the fact that he was dying!

HELEN.   Don't you think he knew that? Why couldn't you just tell him what he wanted to hear?

AVERY.   I just think you should try to tell the truth....

HELEN.   Jesus, lie a little! Say ten Hail Marys and give the rest of us a break...!

AVERY.   Can we go please?

HELEN.   No.

AVERY.   No?

HELEN.   I don't want to be your chauffeur, Avery. I want to be your friend.

AVERY.   Well at this moment, I need a chauffeur more than a friend.

HELEN.   Then call one. *(Helen opens Avery's door, hands her a bag of groceries and shoves her out. Helen yanks the steering wheel out of the stage floor and peels out. Avery calls after her.)*

AVERY.   Helen! *(Avery looks up and down the street, realizing she's stranded. Avery sees the bag of food. She falls to her knees. She takes a bite of the candy bar then wolfs it down hungrily, chasing it with a can of beer.)*

BLACKOUT

Scene 5

The Marina District. Avery and Michael stand in the flick-ering light of a burning house.

AVERY. Why do earthquakes set houses on fire?

MICHAEL. The electrical wires. Sparks. Gas.

AVERY. Are you sober?

MICHAEL. That's a hell of a thing to ask. The polite ques-tion is "Are you drunk?"

AVERY. Are you drunk?

MICHAEL. No.

AVERY. Why not?

MICHAEL. Well you've fairly got me there.

AVERY. I thought....

MICHAEL. You thought, you thought ... I think once in a while too, you know. This is a crisis, you've got to keep a level head in a crisis, got to rescue the cat and bully the insurance agents, save the pumpkin. You have a smudge on your fore-head. It's very Catholic, very penitent, very Ash Wednesday.

AVERY. Is it off?

MICHAEL. Almost. *(He touches her forehead gently. Beat.)* I wish I could read your mind.

AVERY. Everybody wishes they could read minds until they get magical powers and discover people are thinking terrible things about them.

MICHAEL. Are you thinking terrible things?

AVERY. About you. No.

MICHAEL. Who then?

AVERY. Myself.

MICHAEL. *(Gently mocking her.)* Bless me father for I have sinned. I've ordered clothes from catalogs, worn them a while then sent them back for a full refund. When invited to din-ner parties I've asked if I could bring anything only to be re-sentful when they said yes. I switched price tags once when I was very broke....

65

AVERY. That's enough.

MICHAEL. You're a nasty priest.

AVERY. Do you think I'm nasty?

MICHAEL. No.

AVERY. Well I am. I told Gerard it was his fault he was sick.

MICHAEL. Do you believe that?

AVERY. My God, he was dying, it doesn't matter whose fault it was, I was so busy judging him, thinking *he* was prideful, when all the time I was guilty of the same sin.

MICHAEL. Why do you have to call it sin?

AVERY. What would you call it?

MICHAEL. Being human.

AVERY. I'm very hard on people.

MICHAEL. You're very hard on me.

AVERY. See.

MICHAEL. But I respect you for that.

AVERY. People respect me but they don't love me.

MICHAEL. Who doesn't love you?

AVERY. There are very few people who love me.

MICHAEL. How many do you need? *(Beat. They look at each other.)* Why did you come here tonight?

AVERY. I had nowhere else to go.

MICHAEL. That sounds dangerously co-dependent.

AVERY. I do depend on you.

MICHAEL. As long as you don't become an enabler.

AVERY. You're very lingo-heavy tonight.

MICHAEL. Well you see I've been to a meeting. Last night when you were on your little date. How was the date, by the way?

AVERY. He was very rich.

MICHAEL. Rich? *I'm* rich. When I'm employed.

AVERY. How was the meeting?

MICHAEL. They served appalling coffee. In urns. It looked like tea. I made a fuss. I insisted it *was* tea. They talked to me in soothing tones, they said I wasn't really upset about the coffee being weak. So, then I complained about the folding chairs. I said everyone would attend more meetings if there were comfy armchairs. I got a round of applause.

AVERY.   Did you say "My name is Michael and I'm an alcoholic?"

MICHAEL.   No, I said "My name is Dr. Michael Bannon, Genius Boy."

AVERY.   And did that get a round of applause?

MICHAEL.   No, they felt I was resisting, which of course I was, so then I got very down-home and insisted everybody call me Mike. Or Mickey. Or just Mick. Because what am I but a great big Mick.

AVERY.   I think hurling ethnic epithets at yourself is always a sign of progress.

MICHAEL.   Well that goes without saying.

AVERY.   Where are you gonna stay tonight?

MICHAEL.   Here. It's not every night you get to watch your house burn down. I don't want to miss a single ember.

AVERY.   And then where will you go?

MICHAEL.   I'm living moment to moment Avery. I know that's hard for a Traffic Watcher to understand.

AVERY.   You look tired.

MICHAEL.   I'm not tired, I'm haggard. We country and western singers always look haggard.

AVERY.   Why don't you come home with me?

MICHAEL.   Home where?

AVERY.   We could go to Gerard's.

MICHAEL.   Will I have to sleep on a couch?

AVERY.   You can have the bed.

MICHAEL.   Will you be in it?

AVERY.   No.

MICHAEL.   Will you ever be in it?

AVERY.   That depends on you.

MICHAEL.   My hands are shaking.

AVERY.   You can make them stop.

MICHAEL.   What if I can't stop?

AVERY.   You can stop.

MICHAEL.   How do you know?

AVERY.   I need you to stop.

MICHAEL.   Oh Avery, if only that were true.

AVERY.   It is true.

MICHAEL.   You don't need anybody.

AVERY.   How can you say that?

MICHAEL.   You're a self-reliant people.

AVERY.   And you're punishing me for that?

MICHAEL.   I'm not punishing you.

AVERY.   I want you back.

MICHAEL.   You could do so much better than me.

AVERY.   I don't want better than you.

MICHAEL.   Tell me why you want me.

AVERY.   You know why.

MICHAEL.   I want to hear you say it. *(Beat.)*

AVERY.   You're very bright.

MICHAEL.   I'm not bright, I'm facile, and I don't want *adjectives* Avery, I don't want a personal ad, I want to know, Jesus, I want to know why you love me, if you do love me, when I've given you every reason in the world to stop. *(Beat.)*

AVERY.   When I'm with other people it's as if I'm waiting for them to ask me the right question, I have all this inside me but nobody asks, and I can't offer, so I'm trapped with my best self inside, sitting there cool as stone, rigid and dull, but you always ask the question I've been waiting to be asked, and when I'm with you, when I hear you, I can feel myself finally come tumbling out....

MICHAEL.   *(Stroking her cheek.)* You're crying.

AVERY.   Without you, I'd be utterly alone.

MICHAEL.   I think maybe you'd like that.

AVERY.   No, I was alone and I wanted you and I did things to get here that I never thought I'd do, I kissed this ... strange man and ate chocolate and stole a car....

MICHAEL.   You ate *chocolate?*

AVERY.   And I lost my job, stupidly, it was so *stupid,* but I couldn't control it, all of a sudden it was in me, anger and envy and hunger and I was like everyone else ... and I liked it. I didn't feel so alone.

MICHAEL.   You're not alone.

AVERY.   Gerard died tonight.

MICHAEL.   That was very dramatic of him. Exeunt pursued by an earthquake. *(She laughs.)*
AVERY.   Hold me. *(He does.)*
MICHAEL.   Avery Bly on High you've come down from the sky.

BLACKOUT

END OF PLAY

PROPERTY LIST

Empty wallet (MICHAEL)
5 dollars (AVERY)
Cigarette lighter (MICHAEL)
2 salt shakers (MICHAEL)
1 pepper shaker (MICHAEL)
Ice-cream container (HELEN)
Stack of mail (AVERY)
Stack of catalogs (AVERY)
Bag of Cheez Doodles (HELEN)
Head sets (AVERY, FRED)
Clipboard (AVERY)
Glass of water (AVERY)
Magazines (AVERY)
Flowers (AVERY)
Car keys (MAN)
Purse (AVERY)
Singles club card (MAN)
Photograph (MAN)
Mobile phone (DATE)
Candy bar (HELEN)
Bag of groceries (HELEN) with:
      candy bar
      beer

SOUND EFFECTS

Telephone ring
Helicopter
Earthquake
Car alarms

NEW PLAYS

• **MERE MORTALS by David Ives, author of *All in the Timing*.** Another critically acclaimed evening of one-act comedies combining wit, satire, hilarity and intellect -- a winning combination. The entire evening of plays can be performed by 3 men and 3 women. ISBN: 0-8222-1632-9

• **BALLAD OF YACHIYO by Philip Kan Gotanda.** A provocative play about innocence, passion and betrayal, set against the backdrop of a Hawaiian sugar plantation in the early 1900s. *"Gotanda's writing is superb ... a great deal of fine craftsmanship on display here, and much to enjoy."* --*Variety*. *"...one of the country's most consistently intriguing playwrights..."* --*San Francisco Examiner*. *"As he has in past plays, Gotanda defies expectations..."* --*Oakland Tribune*. [3M, 4W] ISBN: 0-8222-1547-0

• **MINUTES FROM THE BLUE ROUTE by Tom Donaghy.** While packing up a house, a family converges for a weekend of flaring tempers and shattered illusions. *"With MINUTES FROM THE BLUE ROUTE [Donaghy] succeeds not only in telling a story -- a typically American one with wide appeal, about how parents and kids struggle to understand each other and mostly fail -- but in notating it inventively, through wittily elliptical, crisscrossed speeches, and in making it carry a fairly vast amount of serious weight with surprising ease."* --*Village Voice*. [2M, 2W] ISBN: 0-8222-1608-6

• **SCAPIN by Molière, adapted by Bill Irwin and Mark O'Donnell.** This adaptation of Molière's 325-year-old farce, *Les Fourberies de Scapin*, keeps the play in period while adding a late Twentieth Century spin to the language and action. *"This SCAPIN, [with a] felicitous adaptation by Mark O'Donnell, would probably have gone over big with the same audience who first saw Molière's Fourberies de Scapin...in Paris in 1671."* --*N.Y. Times*. *"Commedia dell'arte and vaudeville have at least two things in common: baggy pants and Bill Irwin. All make for a natural fit in the celebrated clown's entirely unconventional adaptation."* --*Variety* [9M, 3W, flexible] ISBN: 0-8222-1603-5

• **THE TURN OF THE SCREW adapted for the stage by Jeffrey Hatcher from the story by Henry James.** The American master's classic tale of possession is given its most interesting "turn" yet: one woman plays the mansion's terrified governess while a single male actor plays everyone else. *"In his thoughtful adaptation of Henry James' spooky tale, Jeffrey Hatcher does away with the supernatural flummery, exchanging the story's balanced ambiguities about the nature of reality for a portrait of psychological vampirism..."* --*Boston Globe*. [1M, 1W] ISBN: 0-8222-1554-3

• **NEVILLE'S ISLAND by Tim Firth.** A middle management orientation exercise turns into an hilarious disaster when the team gets "shipwrecked" on an uninhabited island. *"NEVILLE'S ISLAND ... is that rare event: a genuinely good new play..., it's a comedic, adult LORD OF THE FLIES..."* --*The Guardian*. *"... A non-stop, whitewater deluge of comedy both sophisticated and slapstick.... Firth takes a perfect premise and shoots it to the extreme, flipping his fish out of water, watching them flop around a bit, and then masterminding the inevitable feeding frenzy."* --*New Mexican*. [4M] ISBN: 0-8222-1581-0

DRAMATISTS PLAY SERVICE, INC.
440 Park Avenue South, New York, NY 10016 212-683-8960 Fax 212-213-1539
postmaster@dramatists.com www.dramatists.com

NEW PLAYS

• **TAKING SIDES by Ronald Harwood.** Based on the true story of one of the world's greatest conductors whose wartime decision to remain in Germany brought him under the scrutiny of a U.S. Army determined to prove him a Nazi. *"A brave, wise and deeply moving play delineating the confrontation between culture, and power, between art and politics, between irresponsible freedom and responsible compromise." --London Sunday Times.* [4M, 3W] ISBN: 0-8222-1566-7

• **MISSING/KISSING by John Patrick Shanley.** Two biting short comedies, MISSING MARISA and KISSING CHRISTINE, by one of America's foremost dramatists and the Academy Award winning author of *Moonstruck.* *" ... Shanley has an unusual talent for situations ... and a sure gift for a kind of inner dialogue in which people talk their hearts as well as their minds...." --N.Y. Post.* MISSING MARISA [2M], KISSING CHRISTINE [1M, 2W] ISBN: 0-8222-1590-X

• **THE SISTERS ROSENSWEIG by Wendy Wasserstein,** Pulitzer Prize-winning author of *The Heidi Chronicles.* Winner of the 1993 Outer Critics Circle Award for Best Broadway Play. A captivating portrait of three disparate sisters reuniting after a lengthy separation on the eldest's 50th birthday. *"The laughter is all but continuous." --New Yorker. "Funny. Observant. A play with wit as well as acumen.... In dealing with social and cultural paradoxes, Ms. Wasserstein is, as always, the most astute of commentators." --N.Y. Times.* [4M, 4W] ISBN: 0-8222-1348-6

• **MASTER CLASS by Terrence McNally. Winner of the 1996 Tony Award for Best Play.** Only a year after winning the Tony Award for *Love! Valour! Compassion!,* Terrence McNally scores again with the most celebrated play of the year, an unforgettable portrait of Maria Callas, our century's greatest opera diva. *"One of the white-hot moments of contemporary theatre. A total triumph." --N.Y. Post. "Blazingly theatrical." -- USA Today.* [3M, 3W] ISBN: 0-8222-1521-7

• **DEALER'S CHOICE by Patrick Marber.** A weekly poker game pits a son addicted to gambling against his own father, who also has a problem but won't admit it. *"... make tracks to DEALER'S CHOICE, Patrick Marber's wonderfully masculine, razor-sharp dissection of poker-as-life.... It's a play that comes out swinging and never lets up -- a witty, wisecracking drama that relentlessly probes the tortured souls of its six very distinctive ... characters. CHOICE is a cutthroat pleasure that you won't want to miss." --Time Out (New York).* [6M] ISBN: 0-8222-1616-7

• **RIFF RAFF by Laurence Fishburne.** RIFF RAFF marks the playwriting debut of one of Hollywood's most exciting and versatile actors. *"Mr. Fishburne is surprisingly and effectively understated, with scalding bubbles of anxiety breaking through the surface of a numbed calm." --N.Y. Times. "Fishburne has a talent and a quality...[he] possesses one of the vital requirements of a playwright -- a good ear for the things people say and the way they say them." --N.Y. Post.* [3M] ISBN: 0-8222-1545-4

DRAMATISTS PLAY SERVICE, INC.
440 Park Avenue South, New York, NY 10016 212-683-8960 Fax 212-213-1539
postmaster@dramatists.com www.dramatists.com